Emmer Green

Past and Present

from estate hamlet to village to suburb

*This book is dedicated to
the memories of
Bill Goodworth
John Darby*

EMMER GREEN RESIDENTS' ASSOCIATION

Published by MAP READING
www.map-reading.co.uk

First edition published in 2001
Second edition published by MAP READING 2003
20 Kidmore End Road
Emmer Green
Reading
Berkshire
RG4 8SE
No reproduction is permitted without the prior permission of EGRA
© Emmer Green Residents Association

Research by members of the Emmer Green Residents' Association
Compilation and Editing by Margaret Ormonde
Colour Photography by Clive Ormonde©
Mono Photos Local Collections
Typesetting and Design by Map Reading
Printed by
Antony Rowe Ltd
Bumper's Farm
Chippenham
Wiltshire
SN14 6LH

ISBN 0-9534436-6-3

EMMER GREEN VILLAGE IN THE EARLY 1900s   PHOTO HIGHDOWN COLLECTION

An exhibition was held on the history of Emmer Green in the year 2000. The subsequent publication of a book was requested by the people attending it. We have endeavoured to include as much as possible, and check and verify facts and figures carefully. Much of that depends on what has been forthcoming or previously recorded.

Old records tend to be in imperial measurements.
For those unfamiliar, please note:
1 inch=2.54 centimetres   1 foot=30.48 centimetres
1 yard=0.9144 metres   1 mile=1.6093 kilometres

Contents

Looking North along old Peppard Road   G N PARLOUR POSTCARD COLLECTION

Map of Emmer Green 2003

-based on the postcode area

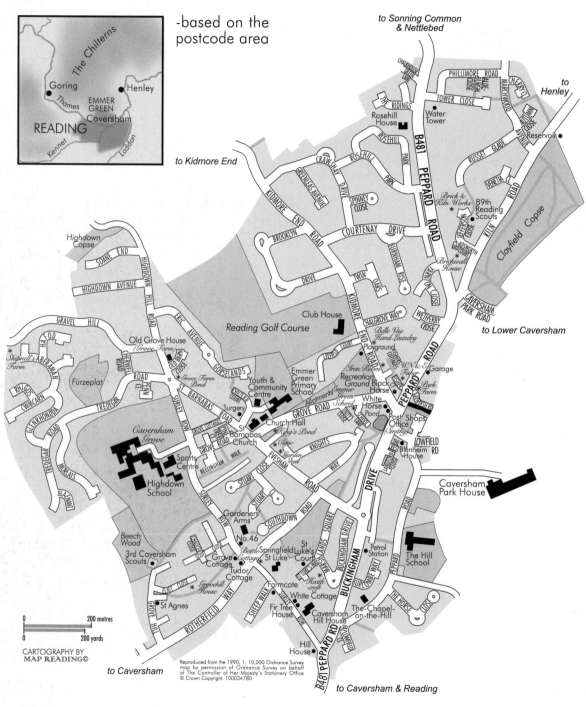

CARTOGRAPHY BY
MAP READING©

Emmer Green ('Emmir Green' on early maps) The name could have originated from an old Saxon word *'Eamere'* meaning 'a lake beside a stream'. The lake, now no larger than a pond, is still there; the stream might be The Swillies which used to run down from Emmer Green pond to Caversham alongside Rotherfield Way. Another theory suggests the name derives from a type of wheat which originated in Egypt, and was brought over by the Celts.

Introduction

Until the late 1930s Emmer Green was a village on its own, quite separate from Caversham. Indications are that it developed as an estate hamlet dependent upon Caversham Park. It had a main pond, and some relatively old buildings, but no ancient church and no central cluster of buildings before the mid 1800s. An old guide book tells us that Emmer Green was regarded as one of the lungs of Reading, and how during the summer months numbers of invalids and those who wanted to be rid of the smoke of the town, descended upon Emmer Green to breathe the fresh air and take water from the springs. Much development and change has taken place since the Second World War, but it is still possible to locate many of the original dwellings and trace their history. The village may have lost its identity in the relentless urbanisation, but with that has come convenience which so many take for granted. There are a thriving parish church, two primary schools, a secondary school, a comprehensive range of shops, and an array of eating establishments.

Heart of the Village

The Emmer Green detailed in this book covers quite a wide area, and is defined by the postcode. However, it is still possible to focus on the original village as being centred around the main pond and the junction of the Kidmore End and Peppard Roads. Quite why the church was built away from the centre is not known.

The White Horse has always been at the centre of village life. It is the oldest inn on its original site, and has undergone internal alterations, but outwardly the building has changed very little. The adjacent smithy and outside stabling remained until the early part of the twentieth century. A row of cottages was demolished to make way for the pub car park. Across the road from the White Horse is **The Black Horse**. This was originally situated on the old Peppard Road, next to Caversham Hill Chapel.

Adjoining the Black Horse was the village bakery run in the 1920s by the Howards. A little further up Kidmore End Road by the entrance to Fishers Cottages was a small sweet shop. The original **Post Office** was part of the bakery until in time it moved to the opposite side of the road. Eventually the former smithy and some nearby cottages were demolished and the present shops built. In 1970 the shopping precinct was built on the opposite side of the Peppard Road, as part of the Caversham Park development.

Blenheim House on the Peppard Road was built in the late eighteenth century, with **West Cottage** an early Victorian addition. A house of character, **Tudor Cottage**, opposite was demolished. From the mid 1800s onwards terraced housing spread from the centre of the village, in a northerly direction up the Kidmore End Road.

The **Emmer Green Parochial School** was built in Grove Road in 1877. A couple of surviving cottages in School Lane date back to the early 1800s. **Pond Cottage**, originally with a thatched roof, dates back to 1563.

The firm of **W N & E Fisher**, carpenters, wheelwrights, and builders, established itself on the Peppard Road, and remained for over a century. **Park Farm**, the home farm for Caversham Park, was situated on land the other side of the Peppard Road, not far from the present shopping precinct. The **Emmer Green Garage** was built on land adjoining the farmhouse.

EMMER GREEN 1986   © READING BOROUGH COUNCIL

1890s

PHOTO FISHER COLLECTION

circa 1940

PHOTO DONATED BY MR & MRS MOULDEN

1990s

PHOTO CLIVE ORMONDE

Landscape & Environment

The district around Emmer Green
is a typical dry valley landscape,
set high above the RiverThames.
Its desirable location was described
in the Parish Magazine of August 1895:
"Emmer Green is a favoured spot,
with views of Nettlebed and Wyfold to the north,
and Finchampstead Ridges and Broadmoor to the south.
Visitors are tempted to call it 'The Alps of Caversham'!"

EMMER GREEN FROM THE AIR 1986
© READING BOROUGH COUNCIL

Geology

A very extensive sea, the Chalk Sea, covered the whole of the British Isles in the Cretaceous Period (70-100 million years ago). Chalk was laid down, ultimately giving us the Chiltern Hills. Chalk underlies the whole of Emmer Green. When the Chalk Sea receded, a gulf was left over what is now the London Basin. Clays and sands, eroded from the emerging landmass to the west, were fed by the rivers into the shallow sea of this gulf. These were deposited and now give us the sands and clays of the Reading Beds (as at Emmer Green), and clays of the London Clay, found in Kiln Road.

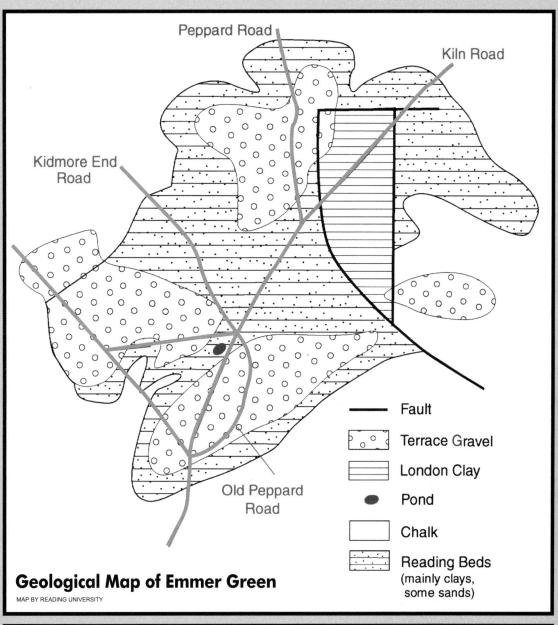

Geological Map of Emmer Green

Peppard Road

Kiln Road

Kidmore End Road

Old Peppard Road

— Fault

Terrace Gravel

London Clay

● Pond

Chalk

Reading Beds (mainly clays, some sands)

MAP BY READING UNIVERSITY

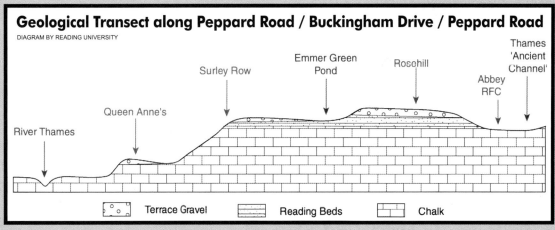

Geological Transect along Peppard Road / Buckingham Drive / Peppard Road

DIAGRAM BY READING UNIVERSITY

Thames 'Ancient Channel'

Surley Row

Emmer Green Pond

Rosehill

Abbey RFC

Queen Anne's

River Thames

Terrace Gravel   Reading Beds   Chalk

Ancient Channel

About a quarter of a million years ago the bed of the River Thames was probably over one hundred feet higher than its present level, and the river flowed over an area just to the north of Rosehill and Emmer Green. This 'ancient channel' lies between from Mapledurham and Henley, crossing an area just to the north of Rosehill and Emmer Green. (It was during that age the Thames deposited on the chalk, gravels and London Clay.) After the Chilterns formed and the Thames settled in its present,more southerly, position these gravels and London Clay were left capping the dip-slope overlooking the Thames between Reading and Sonning. The old 'ancient channel' was a favourite hunting ground for Old Stone Age (Paleolithic) man and numerous flint tools have been found close to it. Further evidence of river depositon can be found in the shape of Bunter Pebbles, distinctive brown, rounded hard stones, 10-20cm across, now found throughout Emmer Green and Caversham Heights. They originated in the Midlands were carried south in the ice sheet, and fed into the headwaters of the Thames.

With the advance of the ice sheet from the north, the Thames was diverted south of Rosehill, through Emmer Green itself. The Thames cut deeper into the Reading Beds clays and ultimately into the chalk. It left a series of steps or terraces as it migrated to the south. These are now represented by flats at Rosehill, Buckingham Drive, and Queen Anne's School, Caversham. Each flat area indicates a colder period when the river was not very erosive, but tended to deposit gravels, like those in the Buckingham Drive area.

Geological Effects

Groundwater dissolves chalk, until the caves which are formed collapse, forming swallow holes. In 1890, at the junction of Kiln and Peppard Roads, near Brickwall House, a hut used one evening for a dance, was next day no longer to be seen, having collapsed suddenly into one of these holes. In 1951 a large deep hole opened up in the ground near Southdown Road. A few years later an unpleasant smell occurred in Comp Wood to the north of Emmer Green. Suddenly with a loud noise a pond soaked away into the ground to be followed later by four mature trees, setting up a great water spout. To this day, holes appear out of the blue, such as those in gardens in Grove Hill in the early 1980s. The photograph shows the caisson being lifted into position to stabilise the ground. The work took a year to complete.

PHOTO IAN FENWICK

Exploitation

The chalk caves in the Kiln Road area were probably in part the result of quarrying for agriculture, or used to line the kilns for the brick-making industry. During the last war, for security reasons, Reading's archives were stored in the caves, in case the Town Hall was bombed, together with cardboard coffins for possible gas victims. There are many underground caves in the chalk around Emmer Green, and in 1977, about 350 feet from the aforementioned cave a new discovery was made down what turned out to be an old air-shaft. Fifty feet under the ground was a cavern with galleries some 30 ft high and well over a hundred yards in length. University pot-holers investigated and found relics left from when the mine closed some hundred years ago. Cart tracks in the mine suggested horse-drawn carts may have been used to transport the chalk from the workings. The mine has been safely sealed, but the main entrance to the cave has never been found. Reading Beds clays were quarried to provide raw materials for the brick kilns in Kiln Road (see p 87). Part of Russet Glade was built in the old quarry.

READING LIBRARY SERVICES

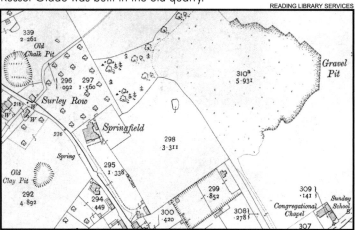

A notable feature of chalk is flint, comprising hard silica nodules arranged along the bedding. The insoluble material is left behind when the chalk disintegrates. Flint gravels were taken out of a large quarry in the area of Marshland Square and Buckingham Drive. Variously referred to as Black Horse Pit, Talbot's Pit and Caversham Hill, it operated throughout the 19th century, finally closing in 1952. The gravel was taken by cart down the track at the rear of the houses in Chiltern Road to the Thames for transportation. Locally the flint was used for roads, walls and buildings. Not a great feature of Emmer Green architecture, but some remains.

Weather

The weather in Emmer Green would have been similar to that of Reading as a whole. Situated well above the flood plain, it has always been spared the serious consequences of heavy rain. People always remember the extremes, and living conditions must have made any cold winters particularly harsh. Records from the 19th century log at the old school show many absences due to the inclement weather, and there are those still living who recall the ponds freezing over enough for them to skate on. This was not without risk however and at least one boy, Gordon Page, who fell though the thin ice on King's Pond, lived to tell the tale. Others were less fortunate, and during a severe thunderstorm in about 1906 three men who were sheltering in an allotment hut near Gravel Hill were struck by lightning. One man died and the others were injured. Photographs survive of a very heavy snowfall on 25th April 1908, but the sun shone on the Sunday, and by the

Heavy Rain on the Corner of Grove Road

29th it had disappeared. The particularly cold January of 1940 was not publicised for fear it may suggest to the enemy the country was incapacitated. There was a series of burst pipes and one Emmer Green household returned from the Christmas break to find water had been gushing from theirs for three days. The snow of the notorious 1962/3 winter came early and was particularly prolonged. By the time Emmer Green Primary School opened after the Christmas break, all the entrances had been blocked and no fuel delivered. Six men had to work all day cutting paths for the entrances to be cleared. School hours were curtailed and the playground wasn't able to be used again until March 1st. The golf club suffered a double blow in 1963. Not only was the clubhouse gutted by fire, but heavy snow closed the course for two months. More recently we have had a succession of mild winters, with the last serious cold spell being in 1981/2 *(pictured below)*.

Summers of the 1930s were hot and dry, particularly in the Reading area, leading people to comment at the end of the decade that the climate was changing. Summers of the mid-seventies and nineties also brought soaring temperatures and droughts. In 1976 as afternoon temperatures in classrooms reached 98°F, the headmaster of The Hill School went against the advice of the education officer and allowed the children home at 1.45pm each day.

After the war many of the open drainage ditches were culverted. Although attempts are made at intervals to clear these drains, they soon silt up again, resulting in mini floods at a couple of road junctions whenever there is heavy rain. Whilst the Millennium year saw a change back to much wetter weather, it is too early to say if this is due to global warming, or a natural cycle.

Emmer Green was on the edge of the gales that affected the south-east of England in October 1987 and January 1990. However it did not escape entirely, and some large trees were toppled, some blocking roads. One bonus was that the fallen cedar trees in Clayfield Copse provided wood for waymarkers *(see p17)*.

The total eclipse of the sun in 1927 is remembered for its cloudiness, but perhaps that is just as well, because children from the old Emmer Green School were led across to the park to view the phenomenom using only tinted glass. The second eclipse of the century in 1999, although not total in Emmer Green, brought with it clear blue skies, and as the crowds had emigrated to the West Country, the recreation ground was deserted, allowing the few who were there with their protective goggles to witness the moment in eerie silence.

PHOTOS CLIVE ORMONDE

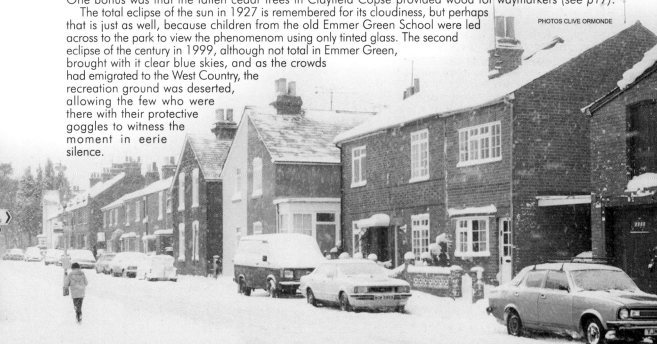

Water

PHOTO CLIVE ORMONDE

There were numerous natural springs (some medicinal) in the area, particularly in Surley Row. The health conscious would visit the chalybeate spring in the Physic Garden in the grounds of Springfield House. It was discovered in1803, and experiments by a Mr T E Williams declared it to be "...saturated to the highest degree with iron held in solution by carbonic gas". In order to make it palatable the proprietor erected a pump to make the water clear and sparkling. Bottled water was sold at Reading and Henley, but recommendations were to drink straight from the pump.

The village pump was not far from the main pond, beside West Cottage (on the site of the electricity sub-station) where there was a source of pure drinking water. It also provided vital water for the blacksmith's forge. There was another supply of spring water in School Lane. The water table was very high and many gardens had their own wells, but the rapid development after World War II made the problem of water supply to the residents a big one. In early 1950 a large reservoir was built along the Kiln Road, and a water tower, 60 ft high with a capacity of 80,000 gallons, was built at Rosehill. The convenience of purified tap water meant the wells and springs fell into disuse.

G N PARLOUR POSTCARD COLLECTION

Vanishing Ponds

Only the biggest of the many ponds (see p13) remains today and it is one of the focal points in Emmer Green. Another small pond close by disappeared when Buckingham Drive was built. There also used to be a pond, King's Pond, opposite the original St Barnabas Church. Sheep used to be dipped in it. Grove Farm, Park Farm and Rosehill Farm all had ponds on their land, but these disappeared in the wave of development that took place in the 1960s and 70s. A large lake near Caversham Park House is still in existence today, but does not have public access.

King's Pond

Grove Farm Pond

G N PARLOUR POSTCARD COLLECTION

Park Farm Pond

PHOTO HIGHDOWN COLLECTION

Emmer Green Pond 1908

PHOTO FISHER COLLECTON

Improvements have been undertaken in more recent years to enhance the aesthetics of the remaining pond, and secure the habitat for wildlife. Early photographs suggest the pond was bigger then, but this seems partly due to the lack of surrounding vegetation. Carts would be driven into the then unfenced pond to allow the wooden wheels to swell around their iron rims, and here too cattle and horses quenched their thirst.

Pond Clearance 1950

READING MUSEUM SERVICES
-BERKSHIRE CHRONICLE COLLECTION

When building commenced between the old village and Surley Row in the late 1940s a serious problem arose between West Cottage and the pond. Drainage of the pond was attempted, to aid development, but as fast as the water was removed, more flowed in. Older residents with wisdom knew this to be an impossible feat as drains had been laid some 200 years earlier to drain the farmlands around. It is thanks to a Mrs Doris Robinson of Chalgrove Way that we still have a pond today, for in the 1960s it was in a state of neglect, and the Council made another attempt to abandon it. She led the campaign to save it and with others introduced and established a number of waterfowl there, including the delightful geese.

Pond Clearance 1990

PHOTO CLIVE ORMONDE

Wildlife

A hundred years ago the natural woodland would have been oak and hazel, with a little bit of hawthorn. Spindle, guelder rose and the wayfaring bush are also special to this area. The diversity of the wildlife in Emmer Green is supported by the retention and management of most of the original woodland areas. By far the most significant is **Clayfield Copse.** The small outlier of London Clay beneath it, which may have helped give it its name, modifies the local soil type and enriches the natural history of the area. Until after the last war, most of the remaining land would have been dairy and arable farmland plus a few orchards. There were also numerous ponds in the area, teeming with aquatic wildlife including great-crested newts. Only one pond remains now, and although it is home to ducks, geese and the occasional visiting swan and kingfisher, it is largely seen as an ornamental pond.

Beech Wood between Highdown School playing fields and the Hemdean Valley, is the only high beech woodland in Reading, and is typical of The Chilterns. Badgers were common and the recent nearby housing development has had to make provision for access to badger setts. The sides of the **Hemdean Valley** were a site of chalk grassland, sadly now lost to housing. The soil in the valley bottom is richer, and not host to typical chalk grassland plants, but there are a few clumps of cowslips which are carefully monitored. **Furzeplat**, further north, has recently been replanted with native species, as part of remedial work for the housing development. A recent survey of **Highdown Copse**, which abuts the golf course showed it to be a botanically diverse woodland with over 60 plant species including box, and the nettle-leaved bell flower. Mature trees include beech, cherry, field maple, pedunculate oak, wayfaring tree, and whitebeam, with no invasive sycamore. Old coppice stools indicate a history of woodland management, and fallen trees play host to a wide variety of insects. The golf course itself has areas of interest,

including a patch of chalk grassland, home to a rare moth. The woodland opposite **Marshlands Square** lies on the site of a former gravel pit, and is predominantly overgrown sycamore, and laurel, with some ash and hazel. A Manpower Services initiative (*photo above*) in 1988 undertook work in these woods, including improving the paths and installing bat boxes. These pockets of woodland are enhanced by old trees surviving in large gardens, and being made subject to preservation orders where necessary.

The wildlife in the area is rich enough to support birds of prey, including red kites, kestrels, sparrowhawks, little owls and tawny owls. These feed off small birds, voles and mice. The red kite, recently introduced to the Chiltern valleys north of Emmer Green, is a scavenger and regular visitor, often soaring over the houses in groups. Several species of bat have been recorded in the area, and the brown and long-eared bats are known to favour older houses. Foxes, rabbits, badgers and muntjac deer are common in certain areas. Grass snakes and slow worms have also been recorded. Despite the decline in the number of natural ponds, newts, frogs and toads are still present. Stag beetles can be found in areas where there are undisturbed woodland stumps.

The two primary schools in Emmer Green both have special wildlife areas with ponds. Mature suburban gardens can certainly contribute to wildlife conservation, and once people are aware of this they can actively promote it. In one such local garden, over the last 25 years, records of 24 (ten breed regularly) species of butterfly and 300 species of macro moths have been kept. Even roadside verges can produce the unexpected, like the broad-leaved helleborines, Emmer Green's very own orchids, in Kidmore End Road.

Clayfield Copse
and
Blackhouse Wood

Clayfield Copse is a mature woodland on the north eastern edge of Emmer Green, on the only outcrop of London Clay in the Reading area, north of the Thames. It covers an area of approximately 8 hectares, and next to it is the smaller Blackhouse Wood. Ancient woodland sites are of prime importance to nature conservation, and parts of Clayfield and the whole of Blackhouse appear on very early maps. In December 1991 Reading's Mayor, Robert Dimmock formally opened Clayfield Copse as the town's first Local Nature Reserve.

PHOTOS CLIVE ORMONDE

15

For centuries woodlands were coppiced, to yield poles for fencing and hurdle-making, and it was an important rural industry. Oak too was in great demand at this time and would be planted alongside the hazel, but allowed to grow to full maturity before harvesting. This type of plantation was known as 'coppice with standards', and there is evidence of this throughout the older parts of Clayfield Copse. The clearance of the woods on a regular cycle was particularly beneficial, sending light through to the lower levels, allowing the flora to flourish, in turn attracting butterflies, insects and birds. Spring is the best time to see the woodland plants. Blackhouse Wood is renowned for its carpet of bluebells, whilst favourable areas of Clayfield Copse support dog's

mercury, sanicle, woodruff, cuckoo-pint, primrose etc. A few patches of the early purple orchid are found in both woods. Whilst trees are predominantly oak and ash, the rarer wild service has also established itself. Autumn is the best time for a fungus foray, and varieties, such as puff balls, Jew's ear, dog stinkhorn, death cap, and honey fungus abound. Twenty-five species of butterfly have been recorded in and around the woods, including the purple hairstreak. The woods are also noted for their nocturnal bat population, and the dawn chorus bears testament to the numbers of birds present. It tends to be rarer to see or hear animals, but they range from small rodents up to the muntjac deer.

PHOTOS CLIVE ORMONDE

It is doubtful whether any farming of the woods has taken place since World War II. Woodlands can stand some neglect, but sensitive management can make it richer and more interesting. In August 1989, at an inaugural meeting between locals residents and **Reading Park Rangers**, a group was set up to maintain and manage the woods for the use of the local community, and for the protection of wildlife. **Friends of Clayfield Copse** (FOCC) was born, and chose to meet on the first Sunday of every month. They worked under the guidance of a Park Ranger and followed the woodland management plans drawn up by Janet Welsh in 1991. These plans are currently under review.

General tasks included tree planting, wood-chipping paths, coppicing, sycamore thinning, bramble slashing and rubbish clearance. Over the years the group has also taken on larger projects. A fence was erected from the entrance to the woods in Kiln Road to Foxhill Lane, to keep the horses out of the woods. A ride through Clayfield Copse, running parallel to Kiln Road was widened. A hoggin path was laid along what was to become the nature trail, and cedar marker posts created by the **Berkshire Woodcarvers** installed along the route. An interpretation board in the car park, and publicity leaflets, both produced by FOCC help promote an understanding of the woods, and encourage their long-term preservation.

In June 2000 the first Woodlands Day was held as part of the Millennium celebrations. It attracted hundreds of people who witnessed various rural woodcrafts, saw birds of prey in flight, shire horses at work and Tamworth pigs roaming free. The Park Rangers have now gone, but FOCC appoint their own task leader. They work under the guidance of Caversham Court Environment Centre (relocated in Prospect Park) and have regular meetings to discuss the forthcoming tasks and projects.

In 1996 Reading Borough Council drew up a management plan to consider the future development of the fields adjoining the woods, with suggestions for sporting facilities in the adjacent field. Nothing materialised from those plans, but the matter is again being considered, after further consultation with user groups. Friends of Clayfield Copse is determined to protect the woodland by keeping these areas as parkland to form an important buffer between the houses and the woods. The continuing dedication of some of those involved in the early days, such as Anne Latto and John Wright have ensured the group's success. It is hoped to attract new members to secure the group's future.

PHOTO DONATED BY JOHN WRIGHT

Berkshire Woodcarvers

The **Berkshire Woodcarvers** had their origins in a small workshop in Grove Hill, Emmer Green. Mr Bill Mander, who retired from teaching in1993, was looking for ways to develop his fascination for the beauty of wood. His family had a long tradition of various crafts involving wood, and so with the aid of some books and carving tools he began visiting woodcraft shows and exhibitions. At one he met one of the national organisers of the **British Woodcarvers Association** who persuaded him to set up a group in the Thames Valley area. There were only four at the inaugural meeting at Twyford in January 1994, but within a year they had begun to take part in local events, often demonstrating their skills to onlookers. By 1996 their numbers had increased to eighteen, some local to Emmer Green, but many from other parts of Berkshire. It had always been the ambition of the group to give their work a more public profile and the breakthrough came later that year when they were approached by Mark Yates of Reading Borough Council to produce a series of thirteen carved way-markers for Clayfield Copse in Emmer Green.

PHOTOS CLIVE ORMONDE

PHOTO DONATED BY BILL MANDER

This provided a new challenge for the carvers as they were working with heavy, large, seven-foot high poles. They were able to use the wood from a Cedar of Lebanon tree that had been felled in the copse as a result of the great storms of January 1990. The massive trunk had been dragged from the woods by a team of shire horses, and was about to be returned in a very different form. The subject matter for the carvings was also taken from the woodland setting, in consultation with local primary school pupils.

PHOTO PAUL GALLAGHER

Snail - Eric Barnes

New Town Primary School provided a suitable workshop, and the funding came from the **Southern Arts Council**. 1997 saw the work completed and the way-markers were installed the following year. Since then they have weathered naturally, becoming an integral part of the woodland scene. The group's relationship with New Town School has continued and the Berkshire Woodcarvers have also produced a series carvings for the Green Gallery of the newly refurbished Reading Museum. As a team the carvers are working on the village sign that will be erected near the pond and depict scenes of Emmer Green, past and present.

Village Sign - Gordon Bennett

Historical Profile

PRE-HISTORY

Some of the earliest evidence of mankind in England is found in Emmer Green and Caversham. It was part of the 'ancient channel' of the Thames and its flood plains, with roaming hunter gatherers using flint tools.

BRONZE AGE

There was some settlement or other site on the plateau around the sites of the present day Old Grove House, Gorselands and Emmer Green Primary School.

IRON AGE

There was continuing Celtic settlement near the site of Old Grove House (Grove Farm).

ROMAN

There was Romano-British settlement around Old Grove House area, with signs of wattle and daub buildings and a metal forge. It may have been occupied for over 400 years, but it is unclear if it was just a small settlement, or something more significant extending to the area on the plateau between the dry valleys of Highdown Bottom and Hemdean Bottom.

MEDIAEVAL

There were no further signs of occupation at the Old Grove House site until the 16th Century. Caversham Manor and Caversham Park estate existed, with the latter being a deer park with hunting lodge. It's not clear whether there was a manor house on the site of the present house.

16th CENTURY

Caversham Park mansion was built in the 1590s by Sir Francis Knollys. Old Grove House and The White Horse inn were built during this period. 16th century coins were found in several locations. Farmcote is thought to be the oldest house in Surley Row. There were some smaller cottages in the area too, some demolished as recently as 50 years ago. Both Tudor Cottages were once several smaller homes, subsequently merged. Pond Cottage overlooking the main pond has a similar background.

17th CENTURY

There were Civil War troops in the area and flint cannon balls were found at Tudor Cottage, Surley Row and in a garden in Eric Avenue. Cromwell was rumoured to have hidden in a tree in Grove Park, and the Earl of Essex stayed at Caversham Park. The mansion was also host to a succession of royal visitors including Anne of Denmark and Charles I. The brick kiln was first mentioned in 1654. No.46 Surley Row (once used as The Gardeners' Arms), and St Agnes (Woodleigh), are flint and brick cottages dating back to this period.

18th CENTURY

Caversham Park mansion was rebuilt in 1723 by Earl Cadogan and his successors. In about 1764 the gardens were redesigned by Capability Brown. Caversham Grove appears on a map dated 1761 and was built in the early 18th century. Rosehill House dates back to 1791 and Blenheim House on the Peppard Road was built as early as 1770 as home of the farm manager of Caversham Park estate.

Brickwall House was built at the junction of Peppard Road and Kiln Road for the brickfield foreman in the early 18th century, has since been demolished. Nos 2 & 4 Surley Row and several larger houses there, built at the end of the century, still stand.

Pride's Map of 1790

PHOTO HIGHDOWN COLLECTION

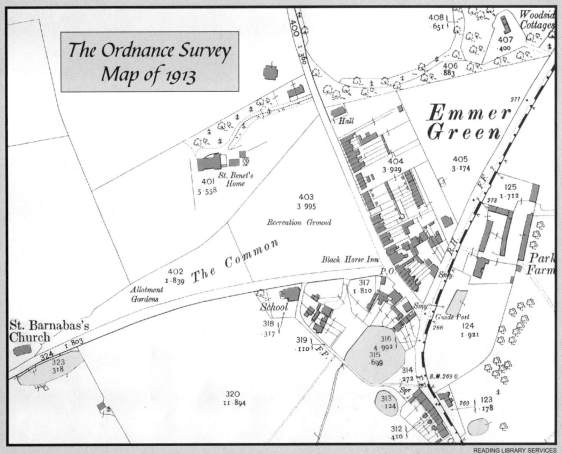

The Ordnance Survey
Map of 1913

Emmer
Green

19th to EARLY 20th CENTURY

By this time the large estates Caversham Park, Rosehill and Caversham Grove were well established, with associated farms and farm workers, servants and their small cottages. The first church (non-denominational) was Caversham Hill Chapel (1827), the school was built in 1877 and the C of E church followed in 1897. The original Black Horse inn was trading by at least 1830, and had moved to its current location before 1870. Cottages which were built near the junction of Kidmore End and Peppard Roads spread in a linear direction. The early 20th century witnessed the beginning of development along St Barnabas Road, and the building of St Benet's Home. Further building programmes took place in the 1920s and '30s along the Grove Road and the Peppard Road. The population of several hundred people grew at a steady pace and with it came a self-sufficient community life, which was to last until the middle of the 20th century.

LATE 20th CENTURY

Post World War II developments were to transform Emmer Green, helping it to become the northern most suburb of Reading, with a population of around 3000. It is now covered with housing and amenity buildings. Open countryside still lies to the north, and pockets of open space remain in recreation grounds, school playing fields, the golf course, and salvaged woodland areas. Most occupants commute to work in Reading, London or surrounding areas. The postcode area has clearly defined Emmer Green's boundaries, separating it from Caversham, but bringing it together with those regions once regarded 'outside' Emmer Green, such as Surley Row and Rosehill.

21st CENTURY

There is very little building land left within the borders of Emmer Green. New development has to focus on infilling, and the hope is that adjacent open countryside will be protected from the insatiable demand for new homes in the south-east of England. Emmer Green is no longer a village, but it is diverse in both its housing and amenities and the character of its population. The hope is that we can preserve and appreciate what remains.

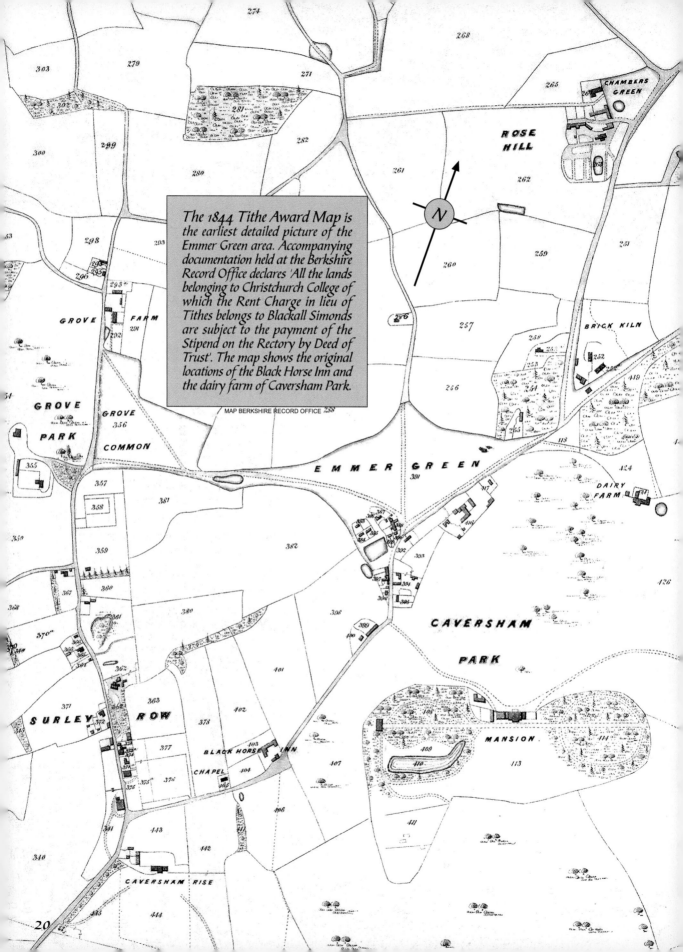

The *1844 Tithe Award Map* is the earliest detailed picture of the Emmer Green area. Accompanying documentation held at the Berkshire Record Office declares 'All the lands belonging to Christchurch College of which the Rent Charge in lieu of Tithes belongs to Blackall Simonds are subject to the payment of the Stipend on the Rectory by Deed of Trust'. The map shows the original locations of the Black Horse Inn and the dairy farm of Caversham Park.

MAP BERKSHIRE RECORD OFFICE

ROSE HILL

CHAMBERS GREEN

BRICK KILN

GROVE FARM

GROVE PARK

GROVE COMMON

EMMER GREEN

DAIRY FARM

CAVERSHAM PARK

SURLEY ROW

BLACK HORSE INN

CHAPEL

MANSION

CAVERSHAM RISE

Pre-History/ Early History

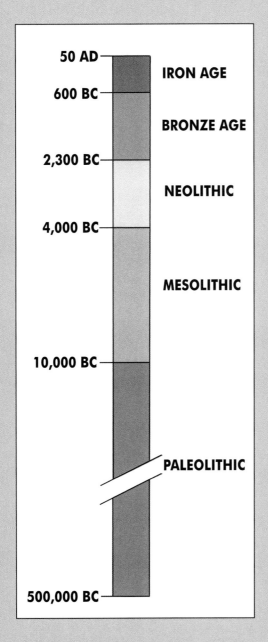

50 AD	IRON AGE
600 BC	BRONZE AGE
2,300 BC	NEOLITHIC
4,000 BC	MESOLITHIC
10,000 BC	
	PALEOLITHIC
500,000 BC	

There is very little written of Emmer Green on the pre-historic to Roman times. Most of the recent development of Emmer Green was completed before there was much interest in archaeology, so surveys were not undertaken or finds were not reported. As early as 1947, however, Mr Duncan Marshall began unearthing relics in his garden at the bottom of Kidmore End Road, opposite the golf course. Over the next forty years he retrieved over 100 artefacts including two stone-age flint hand axes, Roman and 16th century coins and mediaeval pottery. By chance, in 1965 a seven year old boy unearthed parts of a Roman urn in his back garden in Highdown Hill Road, just 12 inches below the surface. That led to finds of Roman coins, more pottery and signs of wattle and daub buildings. Other discoveries from an earlier age, found elsewhere in Emmer Green included Palaeolithic hand axes, various Neolithic flint artefacts, Bronze Age axes and pottery, and Iron Age pottery. Many of the various treasures can be seen in the Museum of Reading.

Palaeolithic

There have been many finds of Palaeolithic flint hand axes and choppers in the gravel deposits around Emmer Green. These are evidence of the earliest human occupation of England in about 400,000 to 500,000 BC. These discoveries are associated with the 'ancient channel' of the Thames, which ran to the north of Emmer Green *(see p10)*. Sites of finds local to Emmer Green include Tanner's Farm Pit, Tredegar Road, Cucumber Wood, Stuart Close, top of Balmore Drive (4 hand-axes were found at Sutton's Pit), Peppard Road, Caversham Hill and Crawshay Drive.

The site at Caversham Hill was a very large gravel pit (several small ones merged), which existed around the brow of Caversham Hill, just northeast of Surley Row *(see O S map p10)* - Buckingham Drive now disects the area. Amongst them were Black Horse Pit, Talbot's Pit and Emmer Green Pit. They were visited by enthusiastic collectors such as Stevens, Smith and Treacher from the 1880s onwards. There are at least twenty-nine recorded finds of flint hand-axes, choppers, flakes, borers and scrapers from the Lower Palaeolithic period of 500,000 BC to 150,001 BC.

Paeolithic Flint Hand Axes found at Hathaway's Pit

Neolithic

Neolithic flint artefacts were found between 1929 and 1933 on Emmer Green golf links at the north east corner of Cucumber Wood. They included flakes, a scraper and a fabricator *(photo right)*.

Neolithic Flint Artefacts   PHOTOS READING MUSEUM SERVICE

Bronze Age

Sherds of Bronze Age pottery are listed in the Museum of Reading as coming from the gravel pits described as Emmer Green or Caversham Hill. Three socketed Bronze Age axes were found during the construction of Emmer Green Primary School in 1951. They were late Bronze Age – 1000 BC to 701 BC and thought to be a travelling bronze founder's hoard, which may have been deliberately buried. These hoards are typically made up of damaged implements, which would be broken up, melted and re-used. Bronze Age pits with pottery sherds were discovered when the houses in Gorseland were being built in 1987.

Three Bronze Age Axes found at Emmer Green School

Iron Age

Sherds of Iron Age pottery are listed in the Museum of Reading as coming from the Caversham Hill gravel pits. A gold coin was found in a garden 100 yards west of St Barnabas Church by a jobbing gardener and bought by the collector George Smith in 1936. The coin, a British Gold Stater coin depicting a warrior, poising a javelin, mounted on a horse is housed in the Museum of Reading, It bears the inscription "TINC CF", this was previously thought to be an abbreviation of "TINCOMMIUS COMMIUS FILIUS" a son of COMMIUS, who ruled the Atrebates from about 25BC to 5AD. However, more recent discoveries have identified the correct name to be Tincomarus. When the sign of The White Horse (*see page 65*) was replaced in the1950s the design was based on the coin. Near Old Grove House some fragments of possibly pre-Roman pottery have been found.There may be signs of a Celtic ditch and dyke fortification, (a defensive earthwork), on the west side of Cucumber Wood approximately around the 200ft contour on the south side of the Highdown Bottom valley. It may extend round Hemdean Bottom to Furzeplat.

Detail of the Inn Sign
PHOTO FISHER COLLECTION

Roman

Sherds of Roman pottery are listed in the Museum of Reading as coming from the gravel pits described as Emmer Green or Caversham Hill. A bronze bracelet dating from Roman times was found at Rosehill Cottage (Burnham Rise/Yarnton Close). In 1965, a garden of a house in Highdown Hill Road near Old Grove House, sherds of a large Belgic urn were found. Thereafter many coarse Romano-British sherds were identified. Excavation was subsequently impeded by neighbouring dwellings, but limited excavation disclosed a pit, a chalk floor and a post-hole. Both pit and the hole produced sherds extending from Belgic to late Romano-British. The pit also yielded fourteen 4th century

Romano-British Pottery found near Old Grove House
READING MUSEUM SERVICE

bronze coins and metal objects, including hob nails, sandal cleats, an iron knife blade, nails, and part of a bronze bracelet. The post-hole yielded an iron brooch of probably before 40 AD. Below the chalk floor were Iron Age sherds, suggesting a pre-Roman occupation. Investigations to find signs of a structure yielded the post-hole and a short length of discoloured soil, possibly indicating a weatherboard or sleeper trench. There were indications of a second, rather smaller post, about 15 feet from the first following the line of the 'weatherboard'. Fragments of burnt wattle marked daub were found in the post socket fill. A further limited excavation, some 100 feet from the first, on the site of new houses in Old Barn Close, gave a shallow pit or part of a ditch, possibly a small burnt-clay floor and small area of collapsed clay wall, and what might have been collapsed wattle and daub walling. There seemed good evidence of another structure with two post-holes and more fragments of burnt daub. The finds included a further sixteen 4th century bronze coins, Romano-British sherds, an iron bit and nails, various animal bones, pieces of millstone grit and much iron clinker. Only one piece of finer Samian ware was discovered and only three possible pieces of Roman tile and brick. The Old Grove House area, therefore, would appear to be a native site probably occupied throughout the Roman period.

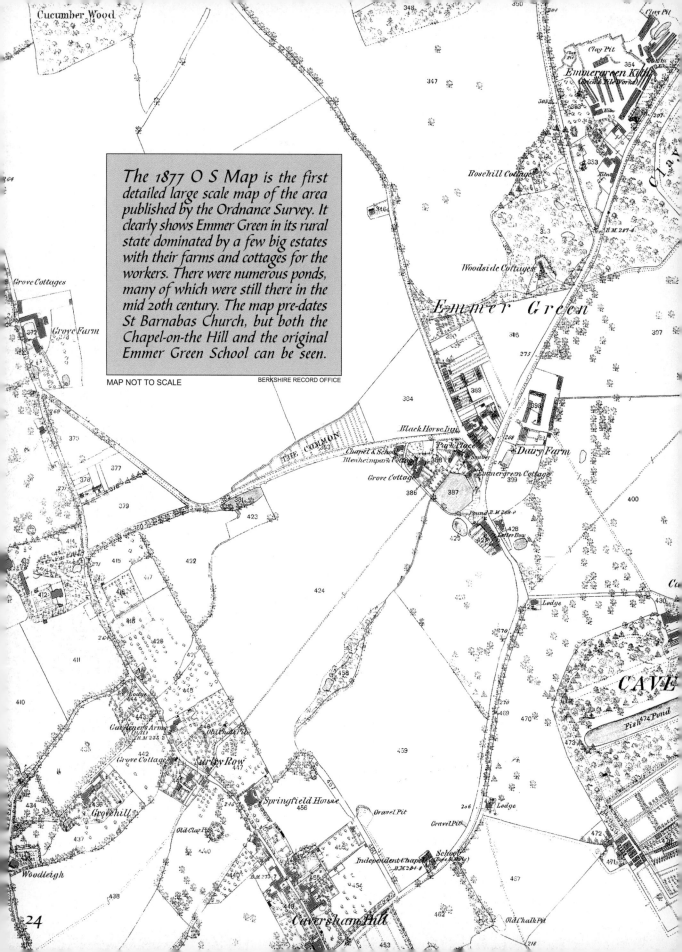

The 1877 O S Map is the first
detailed large scale map of the area
published by the Ordnance Survey. It
clearly shows Emmer Green in its rural
state dominated by a few big estates
with their farms and cottages for the
workers. There were numerous ponds,
many of which were still there in the
mid 20th century. The map pre-dates
St Barnabas Church, but both the
Chapel-on-the Hill and the original
Emmer Green School can be seen.

MAP NOT TO SCALE   BERKSHIRE RECORD OFFICE

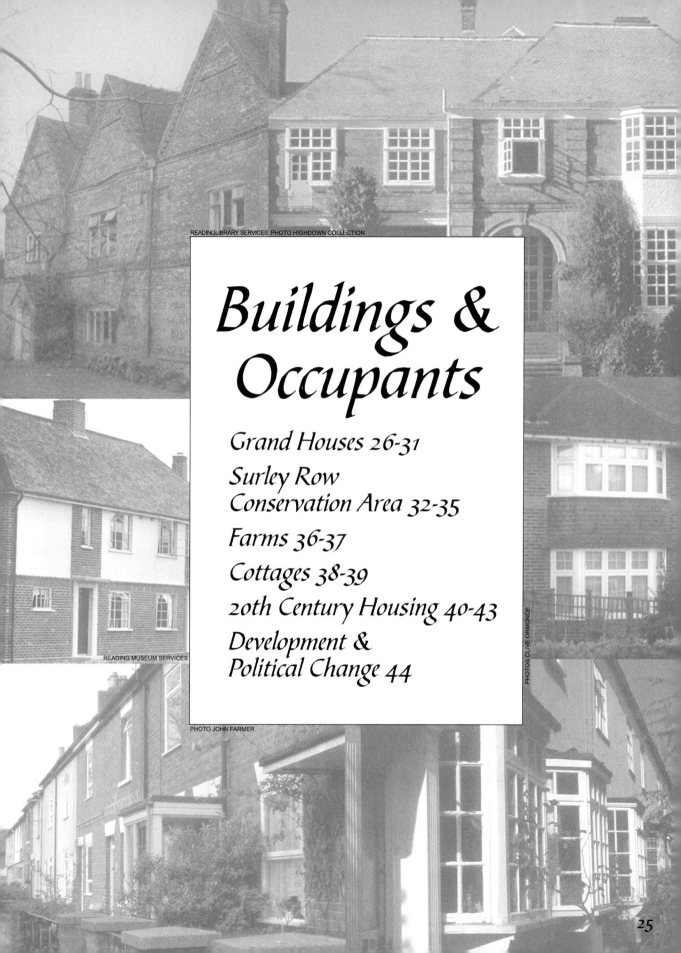

Buildings & Occupants

Grand Houses

There were some fine houses on the land around Emmer Green; the biggest had farms and cottages on their estates. **Caversham Park** has a history dating back eight hundred years, and was the reason the estate hamlet of Emmer Green evolved. The house has been re-built several times, but early owners were of some standing, and royal guests were not unusual. The cottages built on the surrounding land provided homes for workers on the estate, and they in turn needed a network of support. **Caversham Grove** and **Rosehill House** were much later, but they too had sizeable estates. Fortunately all three houses survive, but are no longer under sole occupancy. Neither are they sterile museums, but functional buildings, which although no longer having free public access, do serve the community well. Caversham Park, after a period as a private boys' school, became a monitoring station for the BBC; Caversham Grove was for many years a maternity home before becoming a secondary school; and Rosehill House, once the headquarters of the Salvation Army has now been converted into flats. Other houses of note in the area include **Old Grove House** and some properties along Surley Row. **St Agnes** (Woodleigh) on Grove Hill has very varied history.

Caversham Park 1913
PHOTO COURTESY OF THE BBC

Caversham Park

Caversham Park House (Grade II listed) was by far the most important house in Emmer Green. The Domesday Book records it as having 2,400 acres and a value of £20. The original 'Manor' (location uncertain) belonged to William Giffard, 1st Earl of Buckingham and a relation of William the Conqueror. It was subsequently owned by the Earls of Pembroke, and later the Earls of Gloucester and Warwick. After the death of Richard Nevill in 1471 Caversham Park was confiscated by the Crown. In 1493 the estate was leased to Notley Abbey, which held it until the dissolution of the monasteries by Henry VIII. Sir Francis Knollys acquired the lease of the estate in 1542, and it was he who built the first mansion betweenn 1588 and 1601. His son, William Knollys, Earl of Banbury and Comptroller of the Royal Household, entertained Queen Elizabeth I here in 1601, and she expressed her pleasure at the Masque and dancing organised for her. Queen Anne of Denmark was a visitor in April 1613, and such was made of the occasion that a new entrance was made through arable land to the south of the house. After the death of William, the estate was acquired by Lord Craven. During this period King Charles I was held at Caversham Park and in July 1647 reputedly saw his children for the last time. After the restoration Craven sold the estate to the Earl of Kildare. In 1718 William Cadogan, Baron of Reading and Quartermaster to the British Army, and a friend of the Duke of Marlborough purchased Caversham Park. He attempted to rebuild the house, but died in 1726, and it was left to his heirs to carry on the work. Capability Brown redesigned the gardens in 1764 and created a new drive up from the Henley Road. Mr Charles Marsack became the owner in 1783 and shortly after, Thomas Jefferson, future American President, paid a visit. In 1844 the estate was bought by William Crawshay, the Welsh ironmaster from Merthyr Tydfil. It was described as having a mansion with terraced walk, plantations east and west of the house, a canal and kitchen garden. In 1850 the house was destroyed by fire and he had it rebuilt around an iron frame. The Crawshay family lived there until the 1920s when the estate was broken up and sold. The house was bought by the Oratory School for Catholic boys. During the school summer holidays in 1926 the building was again gutted by fire. The Reading Fire Brigade was first on the scene, but the engines stopped dead at the gates when it was realised the school was outside the boundary and no concern of theirs! The school continued to function until the outbreak of war when the boys were evacuated to Downside School near Bath. Caversham Park House was requisitioned by the Ministry of Health for possible use as a hospital, but was subsequently sold to the BBC and was used as a world-wide monitoring station, from 1943 onwards. A locally recognised fact about the house was that it had 365 windows, one for every day of the year! (Further reading:
Caversham Park and its Owners by *J Malpas*) ISBN 0-9528902-0-8

Dining Room

PHOTOS HIGHDOWN COLLECTION

Fire at The Oratory School, Caversham Park, 1926

Rosehill House

The house, set within a sixty acre estate in the north of Emmer Green, was built in 1791, although there may have been a building here some thirty years earlier. Apparently the estate evolved from a farm, originally part of the ancient Royal Manor of Caversham. The house comprised some twenty rooms, with outbuildings including a range of stabling with clock-tower. The cedar in the grounds was planted by Mrs Elizabeth Richards who owned the property from 1802 to 1837. There used to be a lead pump in the garden bearing her initials and the date 1812. A Mrs Pocock had occupied Rosehill by 1840, and a guidebook described it as 'one of the healthiest and pleasantest places to live near Reading'. Henry John Shepherd bought the house and estate eight years later, enlarging the former, and improving the pleasure gardens. From at least 1875 until 1882 Thomas Rogers, the seemingly beligerent, self-opinionated Clerk to Reading Local Board of Health lived there. In 1878 Mr Rogers had purchased the estate from Christchurch College, Oxford, but he didn't keep it for long, for in 1882 Rosehill House and an estate of 500 acres was purchased by the executors of the MacKensie Estate for £33,550 and let to Mr Martin John Sutton (the seed family). He preferred to call it Kidmore Grange. He successfully bred pedigree cattle, sheep and horses there, served on the council of the Royal Agricultural Society, and was a leading member of the Smithfield Club. He was Reading's Mayor in 1904, and received the Freedom of the Borough. He died in 1913. In 1907 the Rosehill estate was sold by the Trustees and shared between three parties. In subsequent years it was sold off in sections to interested parties and developers. The flamboyant Captain Maitland whose family lived in the house in the early 1900s caused quite a stir when he landed in the garden in his balloon one Saturday afternoon. He died in the 1914-18 War. In 1922 The Oratory School moved to Caversham Park, and two years later, Rosehill became its Preparatory School. For a while during and after the last war the Salvation Army had its headquarters there. From a fire-warden's post on the roof of the building the blitz in London could be clearly seen. It is believed some German prisoners were kept there during the war, as some graffiti was uncovered in the attic. It was later used as a conference centre until the Salvation Army sold it to Haddock's the builders in 1958. The house is now converted into 19 flats, and the remaining 14 acres of grounds developed (Rosehill Park).

Caversham Grove

Caversham Grove (Grade II listed) appears on maps as early as 1761 and the estate at one time included the old Gardeners' Arms in Surley Row. It was built in the early 1700s in Queen Anne revival style, and had stabling for fifteen horses. The cellars are the one curious feature about the house. They contain many rooms, a labyrinth of passages, stairs, and three different ways out! The first owner was Henry Smith who became High Sheriff of Oxfordshire in 1731. His first wife was connected with the Kildares who owned Caversham Park until 1718. The next owner was Captain Arthur Forrest, Commander in Chief of the English Fleet based in Jamaica. It was whilst staying at Caversham Grove that his sister Penelope met, and later married, John Loveday of the Old Parsonage in Caversham (later Caversham Court). Mr David Fell, another High Sheriff was the owner in 1788. He was the man responsible for the election of Lord North (later Prime Minister) and in Easter 1790 he took an oath against bribery. His wife Catherine survived him, but from 1830 onwards the house was let to a number of tenants. In 1878 Mr George Frederick Saunders, Chairman of the Great Western Railway, purchased Caversham Grove. The house was extended on many occasions, the most significant being by Norman Shaw in the late1870s for Mr Saunders. George Saunders died in 1901, and his widow remained there

PHOTO HIGHDOWN COLLECTION

until about 1914. In 1918 Reading Industrial Society had the property, and from then on it was let to various tenants, the first being the wealthy Thaddeus Arathoon who had made his money in India. During the 1920s it was mainly lived in by the Foster-Browns. The house was purchased in 1932 by Reading Education Committee, and was subsequently used as a storage area and general archive depository. Reading Museum kept stuffed snakes, birds and animals there, including a lion, which occupied a space in front of the hall doors. Mr Charles James was the head gardener for the Foster-Browns and he stayed on as caretaker after the house was sold. There were two kitchen gardens, the second being on the other side of Surley Row in the region of the present Gardeners' Arms. Early in the war the Ministry of Health took the house over as The Grove Emergency Maternity Home, mainly for expectant mothers from London, Southampton and Portsmouth. There were several beds in the cellars, a nursery for the babies, and an emergency kitchen. The maternity home continued after the war and by June 1950, the 5000th baby, Sheila Wren, had been born there, and introduced to the then Mayor of Reading Alderman F A Clark. The barn in the grounds of Caversham Grove was made into a small school in the late 1940s. The Grove Secondary School opened in 1952, and by 1970 this had become Highdown School. The recently refurbished house, the tithe barn (which has the design of corn sheaves in its brickwork), the stables, and the kitchen garden wall, are all listed and an integral part of the school.

Etch of Caversham Grove 1761

PHOTO HIGHDOWN COLLECTION

Old Grove House

The former farmhouse (see p37), at one time known as Plaister's Grove, situated near the junction of St Barnabas Road and Surley Row has a fascinating past. Land surrounding the current boundary of Old Grove House has yielded evidence of life in the Bronze and Iron Ages with further occupation in the Roman period (see p21-23). During restoration of the house in the 1960s an old stone floor was unearthed in the dining room, which, it has been suggested could be Roman. The house has a Tudor front of flint and brick, and three gables. Over some windows can be seen brick dripstones, and there is some timber framing at the back of the house (photo right). As late as 1966 there was a building projecting forwards from the the north side of the house. Internally it boasts magnificent original open inglenook fireplaces, exposed timbers, Tudor brickwork and exposed wattle and daub walls in the attic. An old timber barn had a wooden threshing floor.

Life as a farmhouse ceased in 1947 when it was sold by order of Brigadier Shearer. It was described as a "Beautiful old brick and flint Henry VIII farmhouse entirely modernised with 8ft high rooms.........Capital outbuildings including a fine old tithe barn. Excellent cottage. Old-world garden, orchard and meadow-land, in all 23 acres with extensive views from the grounds over the South Oxon Golf Course, which it adjoins". At some point the house fell into disrepair, but by 1964 was owned by the developer Claude Fenton who built Old Barn Close in its grounds. The following years posed an uncertain future. Preservation orders were enforced and allowed to lapse in 1964, and a threat of demolition emerged in 1965. Applications to convert into eating, drinking or entertainment premises between 1964 and 1978 were all fought vigorously. During this period of neglect, it was actually the opposition of local residents and the support of Reading Civic Society that finally saved it. The residents banded together and presented a petition to the planning and building committee, and were granted a stay of execution. Attempts to turn it into a country club, or pub by the Reading based Gainsmead Group were also thwarted, and eventually the Civic Society found a purchaser who bought the house for £100 and with a Ministry grant of £1300 undertook restoration. Since the sale of the property in 1990 it has been continually maintained, creating an excellent family home with great character and modern facilities. The Grade II listed barn was also sold, with planning permission to convert into two dwellings.

PHOTOS DONATED BY MRS JANSEN

Grovehill / St Agnes

Grovehill House, which occupied a prime site with views across the Thames Valley, was built in the second half of the nineteenth century, possibly for draper Thomas Moore and his family. By 1881 he had retired, but with his wife and three grown-up daughters still lived at the house. Towards the end of that century it had passed to a family of Irish descent. Retired from the Canadian Army, Robert Day Hassard occupied it with his wife Margaret. Both families employed servants who also lived at the house. From the late 1920s onwards Brig-General John Crowe C B, a man with a highly distinguished military career, was in residence. Set well back from the road, both house and lodge were demolished in the 1960s to make way for a new housing estate.

St Agnes, the flint and brick cottage with scalloped barge-boards, and hoodmoulds to the windows, is situated at the top of Grove Hill. It is characterised by its ability to undergo change. Even the name is comparatively new, being brought by Miss Dugdale in the early 1930s when she purchased Woodleigh for use as a residential school for disabled and handicapped children. She remained there for thirty years and the name became permanent. The northern boundary of Woodleigh, was much the same as it is today, whereas elsewhere the grounds were quite extensive. Unfortunately the closing and widening of Grove Hill in the 1960s robbed it of its spacious frontage, cedar tree and seat. At one time it was a farm, and in the 1950s the farmer's daughter related how as a child, many years previously, she would lie on the wooden floor of the house to detect the sound of her father's horse bringing him home from Reading Market.

The oldest part of the house is the rectangular flint and brick section on the northern side. The flint, which is of local origin, is less sophisticated than that in the rest of the house, and the walls, which are lined with blocks of chalk are very thick. It is said that it dates back to about 1650, and that it could have been a look-out or garrison guarding the north entry to Reading, and the valuable wool trade. Indeed the cross on the gable is said to indicate Cromwellian sympathies. Cromwell was supposed to have directed the firing of his cannons on Balmore Hill from an upstairs window of the house which gave a clear view of Caversham Bridge.

The Back of St Agnes - the View from the South-east

PHOTOS DONATED BY THE MANDER FAMILY

The part of the house that overlooks Reading now was presumed nineteenth century with French windows and a verandah. However, when recent renovations were underway, some evidence emerged of two Georgian/Regency sash windows and a central floor to ceiling window. With later additions to the house, one of the original walls became an internal wall, revealing marks showing window spaces identical in size and shape to the metal Victorian copies installed along the front. In fact many of the windows were changed to comply with the regulations when the building became a school. The only one left in its original format and location is under the cross in the gable on the ground floor. A wash house with a well used to be attached to the back door area. There is also a cellar under the 18/19th century addition. The stairs however emerge in the old flint section, and the arches and the floor suggest that too could be seventeenth century. The interior of the house is very functional, with no elaborate plastering or woodwork.

The Front of St Agnes (-the Coach House on left)

Surley Row

- was originally one of the main routes out of Reading to the villages beyond. It is likely early owners of Caversham Park House used it to visit Hardwick House. Once a narrow country lane, it has retained its character despite being surrounded by suburban architecture. The whole road, now no longer a through route, from the Gardeners' Arms pub through to the Peppard Road was declared a Conservation Area in 1988. Most houses described are Grade II listed buildings.

No 46 Surley Row *(left)*, a 17th century flint and brick colour-washed cottage with its roof coming down to ground level, was the 18th century 'Gardeners' Arms'. Although the landlord's daughter remained in the house, it had ceased being a pub by 1926. The original settles were in the house until quite recently. Victorian coins, clay pipes and newspapers have also been discovered there. The current Gardeners' Arms was built in 1927 (see p66).

Tudor Cottage at the junction of Surley Row and Rotherfield Way was built in 1540 for a farmer, with the barn being incorporated into the original dwelling some fifty years later, and the addition of two inglenook fireplaces. Timbers from previous buildings were used, as there are two very old carved timbers of mediaeval origin. Flint canon balls used in the Civil War were found in the garden, and have been carefully preserved. A more recent addition to the house has been meticulously constructed to ensure its compatibility with the original house.

Before Rotherfield Way was extended beyond Surley Row, **Bottle Cottage** *(above)* stood diagonally opposite Tudor Cottage. Curiously its front wall was composed partially of the bottoms of old bottles, the remains of which have been found on the current site.

Tudor Cottage & Grove Cottage

Grove Cottage, seen here in the distance is early nineteenth century in a somewhat fantastic Tudor- Gothic style.

Springfield St Luke (*pictured below*) is an imposing white, late 18th century villa with a tented verandah. There used to be a farmhouse on the site. In the grounds is one of the chalybeate springs that gave rise to the idea of developing it as a spa. Once occupied by Sir Rufane Donkin, the founder of Port Elizabeth, and later by Admiral Coffin, the house was in more recent years in the ownership of the Community of St Mary, Wantage. They ran it as a home for elderly ladies until they grew so old themselves that they could no longer cope, and in 1987 it closed. During their occupancy an extension and a chapel were built. The main house has been converted into flats and a new home for the elderly (St Luke's Court) has been built in the grounds. The stained glass windows from the chapel have been saved and installed in the entrance hall of the home.

Farmcote, largely hidden from view, is very likely the oldest house in Surley Row. It was originally a small keeper's cottage built in the early 16th century, and by the 18th century was part of the Caversham Hill Estate, and home to their coachman. Much altered over the years, it once had a thatched roof, like the nearby garage, which has an unexpected origin as a wayside chapel. Signs of the original mullioned windows can still be seen inside the garage.

Byways and The Turrets (Nos 13 and 15) were originally the coach house and stable belonging to The Hill, and were altered early in the 20th century. No 15 has a weather vane in the shape of a hare. It is peppered with holes, a remnant of the days when it was a victim of passing 'young bucks'! One Emmer Green resident recalls living there as a child in the early 1930s and remembers how one night, sheep from an adjoining field broke into the garden and devoured his mother's roses - they flourished the next year!

White Cottage (No 4), is a listed 18th century building, and at one time the blacksmith's cottage. **No 6 Surley Row** was the forge, which served Springfield St Luke when it was a farm and not a gentleman's residence. **No 8**, adjoining, was built in 1750 and once used as the butler's house for the later Springfield St Luke House. Both **No 10** and No 8 (*pictured right in the 1920s*) have cellars, and the 'external' chimney for No 10 is in the hall of No 8. At one time No 10 was home to the head gardener of Hill House, Mr Sidney Gibbs.

Hill House

PHOTO & WALLPAPER SAMPLE DONATED BY LADY DURANT

Hill House and The Belfry, late eighteenth, or early nineteenth century, were originally one house and the grounds extended to the south to cover what are now Picton Way and Balmore Drive. The first owner was Captain William Montague who seems to have been something of a Regency buck, and was one of the Stewards at the Reading Races held on Bulmershe Heath around 1813. Later it was the home of bachelor Mr Richard Hatt Noble, wealthy landowner and influential London banker, who was remembered as a very Christian gentleman in his generosity to local children and staff (see p72). Upon the death of Miss Emma Noble (Mr Noble's niece) in 1930 the estate was broken up and sold. The house was divided and outbuildings converted in 1939 by Paddick Builders. The Adam staircase was removed to another property, but the three Adam fireplaces remain in the house. Since conversion it has had a number of eminent residents including the current occupants, Reading's former Member of Parliament, Sir Anthony Durant and his wife. A bell, once used to announce one's arrival or summon coachmen, is still a prominent feature of The Belfry. The background panel of this page is a copy of a sample of the original wallpaper used in the house.

PHOTO CLIVE ORMONDE

Ladies' Meeting in the Garden of Hill House, circa 1910

Mr Noble and his niece, Miss Emma Noble (see p 62) employed domestic staff who became like members of their own extended family. Miss Alice Hurn recalled the days when her parents were butler/valet and cook in Hill House in the 1890s, and she had vivid memories of the daily grind of everyday life. In spite of the difficulties the house was always open to visitors and gatherings. The Christmas party for friends and staff alike seemed magical to the young Alice - a feast in the dining room (with crackers), a whist drive in the library, and dancing in the drawing room.

Fir Tree House (*photo right*) was built in the 1690s with extensive land, and was once owned by Christchurch College, Oxford. A Victorian bay frontage was added, but removed by subsequent owners. The name of the house relates to the Cedar of Lebanon tree which now dominates the garden.

Caversham Hill House is a late 18th century stucco villa, with an unusual two storey portico and veranda to the south. In 1844 it was owned and occupied by George Cooper. By the second half of the 19th century it was wine merchant Lewis Cooper, his wife Julia and their seven children and four servants who were in residence. It remained in the family until a few years after Julia's death in 1920. By this time the property included adjacent paddocks and a number of outbuildings. It was a subsequent owner Elsie Vaughan who sold five lots of land for building in 1946. The house also became known as the Bishop's House, because it was the home of Rt Rev Arthur Groom Parham, Bishop of Reading. Its latter usage, out of private ownership, has included a home for mentally handicapped youngsters and a nurses' accommodation. One battle Surley Row residents had with the Health Authority was to ensure the surrounding wall was rebuilt in keeping with conservation policies.

Farms

PHOTO HIGHDOWN COLLECTION

There were four main farms within the boundary of the present Emmer Green. Most were run by tenant farmers, some of whom stayed for many years. **Park Farm** (*photo above*) on the Peppard Road was always known to locals as May's Farm. In fact that farm began life as the homestead yard for Caversham Park, and the dairy farm moved there from its original location, not far from Caversham Park Primary School, around 1865. The 1881 census shows Thomas Simmonds, farm bailiff and his family to be living in the farm house. In 1910 the farm is recorded as being of 191 acres, and occupied by Ernest William May. Mr Carey Moore recalls the house from the 1940s. There was the main farmhouse which was double fronted and had a door in the centre. The front garden had a railing painted white which was in a position back from the road some distance, and this marked the property boundary. On the north side of the farm house, and adjacent to the driveway were the servants' quarters and the store rooms. Some chickens were kept in the walled back garden. The 1932 OS map already shows many of the farm buildings had disappeared. A few years later the Emmer Green Garage had been built on the land. The farmhouse remained for many years, until that too was abandoned and finally swept away in the wave of development. Half of one of the barns, which is now used as an artist's studio, and some of the flint walls remain. The main photograph on this page is of **Grove Farm** (*see p37*). The barns on the left were the milking parlours.

PHOTO G N PARLOUR POSTCARD COLLECTION

Most of the estates had their own farms, and just over a hundred years ago **Rosehill Farm** was one of several on an estate that at one time measured nearly 500 acres in size. The Palmer family were the last to run the farm. The farmhouse itself was demolished when The Ridings was built. Paradoxically **Grove Farm** *(left, and main photo p 36)*, near the junction of St Barnabas Road and Surley Row, was also part of the Rosehill Estate at that time. This had not always been the case as for many years much of the land in the area belonged to Christchurch College, Oxford. As early as 1775

Grove Farm was rented by the well known Berry family, farmers and harnessmakers, but in 1832 they were in financial difficulties and were no longer able to pay the college. Early records at The Hill Chapel describe church services held in the kitchen of the farmhouse. The 1844 Tithe Award map shows Thomas Brown to be the farmer at that time. By 1851 James Robert was the farm bailiff; he was followed by Thomas Rumball, and it was Jason Paxman, sporting his marvellous sandy coloured whiskers, who remained there throughout the 1890s until after the outbreak of the First World War. Colonel and Mrs Stevens were the last to farm at Grove Farm, by which time it was no longer part of the Rosehill Estate. The subsequent history of the house is related on page 30. **Shipnell's Farm** *(photo below)*, located at the bottom of the Hemdean Valley, was for many years owned by the Baker brothers, managed by Fred Prictoe, and was the last of the farms to succumb to the demand for housing. For many years, up until its closure a riding stables operated from the premises. For a general account of farm life and work see page 89.

Emmer Green Chicken Farm

The farm's origins pre-date the Second World War, when a nursery garden was set up, complete with two 100ft glasshouses, by the Derry family on land behind 44 Highdown Hill Road. During the war Mrs Derry maintained the business whilst her husband was away and also kept a number of domestic animals. On Mr Derry's return they established a piggery in Gravel Hill, and the house and land in Highdown Hill Road were sold in 1950 to a Mr and Mrs Wallace. They set about converting the premises to a chicken farm, to sell mainly eggs, but some meat. It began on a small scale, but subsequently became a thriving business, supplying not only local residents, but restaurants and hotels in the Reading area. They also had a stall at Slough market. Before it closed in the early 1990s the farm housed 10,000 battery farmed chickens. When the Wallaces retired and moved to Ireland the land was sold to Westbuild Ltd who built five executive style homes in a cul-de-sac called Soane End.

Cottages

Blenheim House and West Cottage

It is easy to forget that some of the early cottages remaining in Emmer Green, most of which have been modernised to make cosy homes, had humble origins as labourers' cottages - damp, overcrowded, and with very rudimentary sanitary arrangements. The original occupants were usually sitting tenants, or the house belonged to their employer, making it a 'tied cottage'. With hindsight one questions why, for a while, there was a trend to demolish anything old, but thankfully things have reversed in the last thirty years, helping to add to the diversity of the area.

Blenheim House on the Peppard Road was built as early as 1770 as the home of the farm manager of the Caversham Park estate. At some stage part of it may have been a village Post Office/shop. The 1877 O S map marks a letterbox very close to the building. It was also run as a school from 1890-1907 (see p 51). **West Cottage**, adjoining Blenheim House, came later, but early records kept at The Hill Chapel show the Misses Mentor and Holdup, two church members, residing there in the early 19th century. Nearby cottages were originally for the farmworkers. **Ivy Cottage** (photo p3) was the home of the Bonner family. Mr Bonner had moved up with the Crawshay family from Wales to work as an office boy. He worked his way up to become an agent, and in one of the rooms in the cottage are rows of pigeon holes where the Crawshay estate papers were filed. There were two very old thatched cottages opposite Ivy Cottage, originally belonging to Home Farm. For many years they were lived in by the Dolton and Angliss families. Mr Dolton was a carter on the Crawshay estate, and Mr Angliss a carpenter. A Mr Budd bought these two thatched cottages and converted them into one dwelling called **Tudor Cottage**. This delightful house, pictured below, was demolished in 1939 (see p67).

A couple of surviving cottages in School Lane date back to 1825. In the 1920s one was occupied by the local blacksmith Mr David Turner, and in the adjoining house local policeman PC Jack Parker lodged with a Mrs Gibbs. Two small cottages behind the pond, each with four rooms and a thatched roof (photo p13) date back to 1563. They were rescued and painstakingly restored into one dwelling, **Pond Cottage** (left), by builder Arthur Akerman in the early 1960s. The meticulous reconstruction included replacing the thatch (photo p13) with hand-made roof tiles.

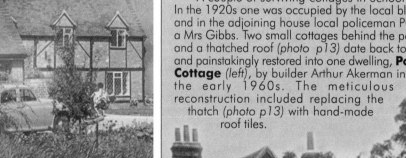

Kidmore End Road circa 1908

There were cottages next to The White Horse called the **White Horse Cottages**. Adjoining the back garden of The White Horse used to stand a very old thatched cottage, at that time, the first house in Grove Road. The last occupants were Mr and Mrs Fidler and when widow Mrs Fidler died in the 1940s it was demolished to make way for the car park.

It was probably after the 1865 'inclosure award' and relocation of The Black Horse, in the second half of the 19th century that the development of housing on the eastern side of Kidmore End Road began. The 1877 O S map shows most cottages had been built from the junction with the Peppard Road, up to what is now number 52. Also built were the northernmost five **Fisher's Cottages**, originally called Baigent's Cottages. Over the next few years building continued along the Kidmore End Road right up to the laundry which opened in 1878. Some of the gardens were very long enabling the tenants to keep pigs, and grow their own vegetables. Even in some of the smaller dwellings there were families with many children, but there was no doubt a spirit of co-operation within the households and neighbourhood, and somehow they managed. The families often remained in the same house throughout their lives, perhaps passing it on to a son or daughter. There are still a few examples of this, but the trend over the last twenty years has been for a more transient population to move in. Today's occupants are benefitting from government grants that were available in the early 1970s to renovate properties and install basic requirements.

Grove Cottages There must have been a similar situation on the area of Grove Common, which was the triangle of land between Grove Road, St Barnabas Road and Surley Row. It wasn't until the second half of the 19th century that building began. Cottages now numbered 18-24 were the first, built by Mr Saunders for his estate workers. The walls of these are now rendered, but an interesting observation was made when repairs were being undertaken several years ago. It was noticed that a large amount of old, dressed stone had been used at the corner of the dwelling nearest the road. Apparently it had come from the old mansion at Wyfold Court when alterations were being carried out. No 24, one of the original ones built by Mr Saunders for his workers, was lived until recently by Mrs Rawlings a descendent of the original tenant.

The two cottages photographed right in 1908 were located at the top of Gravel Hill. One was the home of the Hunt family (see p 78), Mr Hunt being farm baliff for Mr Saunders of Caversham Grove. They were demolished in the 1970s.

20th Century Housing

Apart from following national trends, the development of Emmer Green was affected by the fact that until 1911, the entire area as we know it today, together with Caversham, was still part of Oxfordshire. It had been part of Caversham Urban District Coucil since that was set up in 1894, but pressure to be incorporated into Reading Borough was resisted for the next seventeen years, partly because the rates were substantially less. When the agreement finally came (with financial concessions), interestingly Mr Crawshay of Caversham Park opted to remain in Oxfordshire, hoping to protect his estate from future development.

Auctioneer's Map of 1907

By 1906 the Rosehill Estate dominated the area, occupying not only over a third of Emmer Green, but stretching way beyond. Over the following years parcels of land began to be sold off, and the first development was along what is now St Barnabas Road. These were spacious Edwardian properties with generous gardens.

It was after the First World War, in the 1920s, when the firm of W N & E Fisher had established itself as builders, that development took place along Grove Road and Peppard Road (*photo below*).

The 1930s saw a major new development on the former Rosehill Estate by Reading builders R J Haddock Ltd. The freehold price of a detached house (*sketch below*) was £950, and the development mostly attracted successful Reading business people.

An advertisement in 1935 for a house on Brooklyn Drive on the new Links Estate described it as "....a detached house with brick built garage, which even the most discriminating home seeker would be proud to own." Building continued up Courtenay Drive and part of Burnham Rise, but it was about to be interrupted by war again.

SUPPLIED BY D A ROBBINS

Rotherfield Way now falls within the postcode area of Emmer Green. At one time it was a country path leading down towards Caversham, with a stile at the top where it met Surley Row. A building initiative there in the 1950s made national newspaper headlines for the ingenuity and dedication of those involved. The shortage of family accommodation had become acute after the war, and it was twelve pioneers who, fed up with waiting on the council housing list, took the bold decision to build their own homes. Much thought and planning was involved, and in 1949 with the encouragement of Councillor Mander, and co-operation with the local housing authority, they formed the **Reading Family Housing Association Ltd**. Membership was limited to fifty, who had to sign a comprehensive working agreement and contribute an initial £25 towards the costs of tools and materials. The estimated cost of building twenty-five pairs of semi-detached houses was £37,000 and collectively they borrowed money from the local authority under the 1936 Housing Act. Some of the volunteers were skilled tradesmen, but the team also included an engine driver, fireman, window cleaner etc. Work was carefully monitored and targets set. As deadlines neared they even set up floodlights to enable them to continue working after dark. Their efforts attracted people from all over the world, and a visitors' book was started. Originally the houses belonged to the association, and were for letting purposes only. In 1960 Reading Corporation agreed to sales to sitting tenants, thus enabling the original loan to be repaid.

PHOTO READING MUSEUM SERVICES - BERKSHIRE CHRONICLE COLLECTION

Rosehill Park in the 1960s

READING LIBRARY SERVICES

Building of Lyefield Court in the 1980s

PHOTO CLIVE ORMONDE

Such was the demand for housing after the Second World War that the Council were anxious to undertake an extensive building programme, and land belonging to Old Redingensians Rugby Football Club, off Grove Road was deemed a suitable site. It was eventually purchased in 1948 (see p93) and building began the following year. The estate, between Grove Road and Buckingham Drive was built of such quality and design that it was used as an example for others.

R J Haddock Ltd, builders, who were already engaged in the pre-war development in the north of Emmer Green, continued to build on land from the former Rosehill Estate. In the early 1950s development extended beyond Courtenay Drive, to Crawshay Drive and Spinney Close. Many of the people who moved there came from other parts of Reading to bring up families. They either had jobs in the town or commuted to London. A few original occupants still live there fifty years later. The final phase by Haddock's on the Rosehill Estate was when the mansion and the remaining 14 acres of land were sold in 1958, enabling Rosehill Park to be built in the early 1960s. Haddock's always had a reputation for quality which was largely due to their director and architect the late Peter Sherbourne. Liked and respected by his workmen, he was out in all weathers to make sure everything was just right.

Building programmes continued elsewhere in Emmer Green throughout the nineteen sixties and seventies, both private and local government initiatives. In the early eighties the new concept of sheltered housing for older residents emerged, and it was then that places such as Wordsworth Court, Lyefield Court, Unity Court and Fisher's Court were developed. Apart from building in the Hemdean Valley, this really only left pockets of land for infilling. The demand for housing is as great as it ever has been, and with property prices still escalating, the tendency to grab every available space, however controversial, is bound to continue.

Hemdean Valley

The **Hemdean Valley**, or Bugs Bottom as it is known locally, was the last remaining piece of open farmland in Emmer Green. It was in a unique position, offering a taste of the countryside within walking distance of Reading town centre. The local people of Emmer Green and Caversham, under the umbrella of their respective residents' associations, together with Reading Borough Council vigorously opposed any development. The first planning application by Higgs and Hill to build 500 houses was turned down causing the firm to appeal the following year. At the end of 1985 there was a public enquiry and eighteen months later the

PHOTO DONATED BY BILL GOODWORTH

recommended permission to build was granted. In January 1989 Nicholas Ridley, the Secretary of State for the Environment endorsed that decision, leaving Reading Borough Council to take it to the High Court. They were unsuccessful, so applied to the Court of Appeal in 1990. Throughout this period there were high profile campaigns and demonstrations by local people, but the builders were equally determined, and continued to come back with revised applications. Unfortunately, because of a change in the law Reading Borough Council were forced to withdraw from the Court of Appeal, and the builders seized their chance to press ahead. However by then the plans had been modified, and great attention was paid to detail on such things as retaining hedgerows and accommodating wildlife. Building was actually underway by the mid nineteen nineties with a promise of minimal disruption to residents in the vicinity. Not everything went according to plan, but now that construction is complete and the houses occupied we have to move on and appreciate what little we still have. Doubtless the new residents of the Hemdean Valley would be equally vociferous if any attempt was made to spoil the small swathe of open land that remains.

PHOTO CLIVE ORMONDE

Development & Political Change

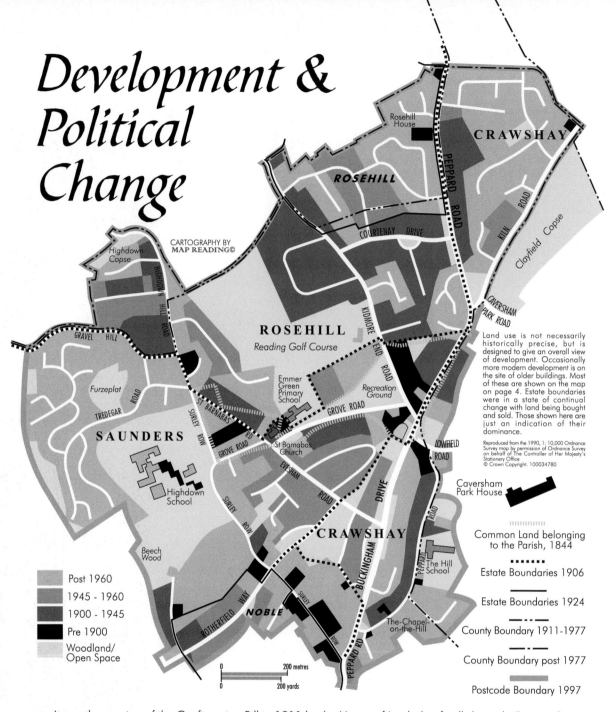

CARTOGRAPHY BY
MAP READING©

CRAWSHAY

ROSEHILL

Rosehill House

PEPPARD ROAD

KILN ROAD

Clayfield Copse

COURTENAY DRIVE

CAVERSHAM PARK ROAD

Highdown Copse

HIGHDOWN HILL ROAD

ROSEHILL
Reading Golf Course

KIDMORE END ROAD

GRAVEL HILL

Furzeplat

TREDEGAR ROAD

SAUNDERS

SURLEY ROW

Emmer Green Primary School

Recreation Ground

St Barnabas Church

St Barnabas Rd

GROVE ROAD

GROVE ROAD

EVESHAM ROAD

LOWFIELD ROAD

Highdown School

SURLEY ROW

BUCKINGHAM DRIVE

PEPPARD ROAD

CRAWSHAY

The Hill School

Beech Wood

SURLEY ROW

NOBLE

ROTHERFIELD WAY

SURLEY ROW

PEPPARD RD

The Chapel-on-the-Hill

Land use is not necessarily historically precise, but is designed to give an overall view of development. Occasionally more modern development is on the site of older buildings. Most of these are shown on the map on page 4. Estate boundaries were in a state of continual change with land being bought and sold. Those shown here are just an indication of their dominance.

Reproduced from the 1990, 1: 10,000 Ordnance Survey map by permission of Ordnance Survey on behalf of The Controller of Her Majesty's Stationery Office
© Crown Copyright. 100034780

Caversham Park House

Common Land belonging to the Parish, 1844

Estate Boundaries 1906

Estate Boundaries 1924

County Boundary 1911-1977

County Boundary post 1977

Postcode Boundary 1997

Post 1960
1945 - 1960
1900 - 1945
Pre 1900
Woodland/ Open Space

0   200 metres
0   200 yards

It was the passing of the Confirmation Bill in 1911 by the House of Lords that finally brought Emmer Green into Reading Borough and the County of Berkshire. From 1948 onwards Reading made several more attempts to extend their boundary further northwards, and this became ever more imperative as development expanded creating anomolies, such as that in Spinney Close, where one side of the road was in Oxfordshire and the other in Berkshire - each with a different refuse collection day! Major revision of Reading's boundaries took place in 1977, and Berkshire acquired the remaining built up areas of Rosehill, Highdown Hill Road, and Caversham Park. A small area to the north of Phillimore Road became part of Oxfordshire.

In local politics Emmer Green originally formed part of the Caversham West Ward, which included Caversham Heights and the Hemdean Valley. In 1958 this was re-named as the Thames Ward. Rosehill was brought into Thames Ward, but it wasn't until 1983 that Emmer Green was detached and added to Caversham Park and Micklands, to be known as Peppard Ward. This was to have a major impact on the political representation. Traditionally a Conservative territory, it then swung in the direction of its new Liberal partners creating a potentially marginal seat. However despite a brief by-election success in 1986, it wasn't until 1994 that Ian Fenwick, Liberal Democrat, displaced Geoff Canning who had served Emmer Green for 15 years.

JENNINGS BROS.

Community Establishments and Support

St Barnabas Church

Until relatively recently (1989) Emmer Green did not have its own parish church, and had been part of Caversham Parish. During the late 19th century the church gathered for worship in the village school, but it was felt a more permanent and appropriate meeting place was needed.

The old St Barnabas Church, the 'Iron Church' (now the church hall), was dedicated by the Lord Bishop of Reading on 17th June 1897. For a while the name of All Saints had been considered, until it was realised this could be confused with the church at Dunsden. Funds were raised locally, and the building itself cost just £410, out of a total expenditure of £715. The first recorded AGM took place on 1st May 1917, the meeting being chaired by Rev D W Jenkins, the Priest-in-Charge. Accounts for the following year show income/expenditure at just over £100, with roughly twenty pounds going to charities and overseas missions.

The choir was photographed in 1908 with the Rev J E Howe, and the other picture shows the inside of the church in the same year.

PHOTO HIGHDOWN COLLECTION

PHOTO FISHER COLLECTION

St Barnabas has never had a graveyard. Two teams of six pall bearers would carry the coffin on their shoulders down what is now Rotherfield Way to St Peter's in Caversham for burial. This was known as Coffin Way or Church Way.

PHOTO FISHER COLLECTION

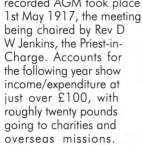

In the 1920s local people, encouraged by a £1000 bequest from the late Mrs Saunders of Caversham Grove, and led by Mr and Mrs Haydon-Bacon, and the Foster-Browns of Grove House, eventually raised enough money for a new church (final cost £2200). The foundation stone was actually laid by Mr C E Keyser in 1924, with the dedication service conducted by Dr W. W. Longford, Rector of Caversham, and attended by the Archdeacon of Berkshire, Rev R Wickham. Three designs were selected, and the parishioners voted for that of the architect Mr J H Willett. It was built by W N & E Fisher, local builders, from old English multi-coloured brick, with red hand-made tiles. The Dedication of the Nave and temporary Sanctuary was held in June 1925, by the Bishop of Reading, followed by the Dedication of the West Window in September 1925, and finally consecration in 1929 by the Bishop of Oxford. The east and west windows in the church were designed by Mr Percy Haydon-Bacon (church warden), a resident of Springfield St Luke and a Fellow of the British Society of Master Glass Painters. His work was renowned both home and abroad with perhaps his most notable contribution being the rose window of the cathedral in Victoria, British Columbia. He actually donated the east window, whilst the west window was financed by Miss Turner in memory of her sister, and another by Mr Bonner in memory of his son. Mr John Hill donated the organ.

St Barnabas Church 1929

Church Choir in 1929 with Rev Morris, Mr Haydon-Bacon & Mr Bonner

AGM reports from 1929 onwards indicate the activities and progress of the church right up to the present day. It was only during the Second World War that social and fund-raising events were suspended. The 1941 AGM questioned whether the church and hall were fully protected against air-raids. In 1945 a church fellowship was formed to help forward the interest and work of the church. There are currently four such fellowships. Sunday School for children was held at the old Emmer Green School until 1933. In the 1920s there were Sunday School outings to Balmore Park, and occasionally more exciting trips by steamer to Marlow or Wallingford *(photo left)*. Now called Junior Church, children attending still meet weekly in the Church Hall for their own service and instruction.

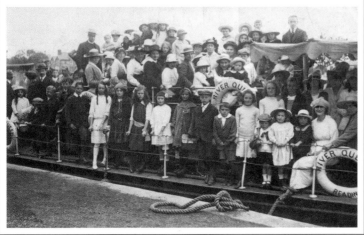

Fifteen Priests-in-Charge followed the Rev Jenkins, most staying for just a few years, then St Barnabas was finally appointed its first vicar in 1989. The Reverend Nigel Hardcastle together with his wife June (who taught at the adjacent primary school) worked very hard over the next ten years and were well liked and respected by parishioners and the community as a whole. Improvements to the building were undertaken in 1995, including a newly tiled roof, resurfaced floor, and replacement of the pews with upholstered seating. Some eighty years after the first AGM income/expenditure has risen to £50,000, and both the Church and the Church Hall are financially self-supporting. In May 2000 the Reverend Derek Chandler and his family were welcomed to Emmer Green.

Replacing the Roof in 1995

Reverend Nigel Hardcastle

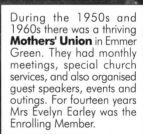
Caleb Smith laying the Path

During the 1950s and 1960s there was a thriving **Mothers' Union** in Emmer Green. They had monthly meetings, special church services, and also organised guest speakers, events and outings. For fourteen years Mrs Evelyn Earley was the Enrolling Member.

PHOTOS BY OWEN JEWISS

Organist Richard Jackson

Caversham Hill Chapel

Caversham Hill Chapel, or the **Chapel-on-the-Hill**, in the Peppard Road is Emmer Green's oldest church. It was started through the Ministry of James Sherman, the Pastor of Castle Street Chapel in Reading, as one of several 'stations' set up in villages around Reading to serve the needs of local people. Until then they often relied on the skills of gifted laymen preaching in farmhouse kitchens. (Grove Farm was one such place). The chapel was built in 1827 with a tower of Bath stone, on land donated by farm landowner Mrs Burchett. She also left an endowment of £1500, the interest of which was used to supplement the Minister's salary. Mr J Dixon was the first Minister-in-Charge. It has the smallest graveyard in England. The sole grave belongs to James Dadswell, a minister at the chapel from 1842 until his death in 1865.

G N PARLOUR POSTCARD COLLECTION

The Chapel-on-the Hill and the Manse

Behind the chapel building was a schoolroom for elementary weekday schooling and Sunday religious education. Pastor Walter Fordham 1866-1883 recorded in the church minutes that £1 per annum was paid for coal for the day school and 4/- per month for clothing for the children. The school finally closed in 1877.

Reverend Robert Lockhead was pastor from 1924-1952. A feature of his ministry was his special evangelistic efforts in the 1930s by way of missions, some held in a tent sited in The Horse Close.

In June 1977 special services were held to celebrate the 150th anniversary of the church. Today Caversham Hill Chapel is a thriving, busy church led by the Reverend Crispin Fairbairn, with a full congregation for Sunday meetings and groups and clubs to suit all.

PHOTO CLIVE ORMONDE

CAVERSHAM HILL
CONGREGATIONAL CHURCH

YOU ARE INVITED
TO
Special Tent Services
conducted by

Rev. ALFRED MATHIESON, London

In Tent situated at Horse Close, Peppard
Road, Caversham, Reading

(Buses from Reading to Emmer Green stop)
(outside gate of field where Tent is situated)

1st to 14th May, 1933

St Benet's Home

St Benet's Home in Kidmore End Road was opened in 1902 by Dr Powell, of Derby Road, as a home for twenty-five orphaned boys, who were then taught on the premises. In the early days it was government policy for many of the boys to emigrate to Canada. Mr Fisher taught the boys woodwork, and each lad had to make his own box ready for departure. Mr Johnson, one of the masters used to escort them to Canada and return for the new school term in September. Tragically many of these young men were killed serving their country in the Great War. The family of Fred Hinton received a letter from, Mr Swann the Master at St Benet's, to say that he was one of seventy 'old boys' who had made the supreme sacrifice. At one time Mr Hill a wonderful gardener at St Benet's grew enormous melons in his greenhouse. Two cottages at the end of the drive housed the gardener and the local policeman. A current resident of Emmer Green recalls life there in the late 1920s, when Mr Twitchen was superintendent, as being very harsh, but the children were already integrating into the local community and attended Emmer Green School. Many went on to serve their country in the Second World War. Mr Flood was in charge during that period and it was he who guided the boys to safety when the Second World War bombs fell *(see p 116)*. Mr Johnston was the last superintendent, and after the home closed he remained in the area, still visited by some of his 'boys'. In latter years the home was run by The Church of England Children's Society. It eventually closed and remained empty for a while, before being demolished in 1982 to make way for a retirement development, Lyefield Court.

Schools

Emmer Green Parochial School 52-53

Emmer Green Primary School 54-55

The Hill School 56-57

The Grove Secondary School/ Highdown School 58-59

The Chapel-on-the-Hill was the first to provide daily education, but the first proper school, called **Emmer Green Parochial School**, opened in 1878 for local children up to the age of thirteen. There was a small private school at Blenheim House on the old Peppard Road. This was started by a Mrs Ayres and continued by a Mrs Jenkinson (1890-1907). There were about twelve pupils and a few boarders. From 1933 until November 1940 there was no school run by the authorities. Mrs Bastin of 244 Pepard Road ran a small private kindergarten, and during the war she was recognised by the Oxford Education Services in order to extend her care to evacuees in the area. Between 1940 and 1948. **St Barnabas Church Hall** was used for school purposes and the classrooms were divided by a big green curtain. Two teachers during that period were Miss Fisher and Miss White. The school was linked to the school in Hemdean Road run by Mrs Webb. Any boy needing the cane had first to walk to the other school in order to collect it! From 1948-1952 the children in Emmer Green were accommodated for their lessons in the tithe barn in the grounds of Caversham Grove House. In 1950 **The Hill School** was built in the Peppard Road, followed soon afterwards by **Emmer Green Primary School** in Grove Road. Both schools take local children from the age of five to eleven years. In 1952 a school opened at Caversham Grove called **The Grove Secondary School**. In 1970 this became **Highdown School**, a comprehensive for children from Emmer Green, Caversham, and north Reading. Pre-school facilities have been available for local children since the early 1960s, first meeting at St Barnabas Church Hall. Twenty years later they moved to the Youth and Community Centre, where they have remained, currently offering eight sessions a week, with up to thirty children at a time. All the staff are local, some serving nearly twenty years.

Emmer Green Schoolchildren in St Barnabas Church Hall

Emmer Green Parochial School

In 1866 legislation laid down that in principle all children should receive education, and in 1880 school attendance became compulsory up to the age of ten. It was probably against this background that the 'Emmer Green Parochial School' opened on 7th October 1878. It was built of brick and flint, situated on the corner of School Lane and Grove Road, had two rooms, a lobby, and boys & girls 'offices' (toilets) and was divided into two sections, infants and 'mixed'. In 1912, with the extension of the Borough, the school was transferred to the control of Reading Education Committee.

Emmer Green Parochial School

Education here was not entirely free and there is reference in the school log to children forgetting their 'pence', and of parents reacting unfavourably to requests for payment towards books. The accounts for the first year show that the school was principally financed by a government grant of £36 10s 6d, by donations from local 'subscribers' totalling £31 18s 0d and by the scholar's pence: £38 18s 8d. Mary Seward, mistress received £17 10s 0d per quarter, her assistant Miss Symes received £6 5s 0d a quarter, and the monitress a mere £1 6s 0d per quarter. A list of subscribers for 1879 included Mr R H Noble, Mrs Isabella Crawshay, Mr Frederick Saunders, Admiral Coffin, Captain D Hall, Reverend J Bennett, and about a dozen others.

One hundred and seven children were admitted on the first day, and from the beginning the school was thought to be overcrowded. As the figures grew several children were transferred to Dunsden Green School and to Caversham Parochial School. There was an inspection by HM Inspector each year and in 1885 his report said at least eight square feet must be provided for each child. By 1886 he was getting firmer: by 1887 the enlargement was carried out at a cost of £76 19s 11d for the building work.

1895

Miss Seward resigned at the end of 1882, probably to get married, was replaced by Mary Hall, who in turn was followed by Miss F Cooke in September 1896. The weather in the winter was often severe, and there are many references to snow causing great reductions in attendance. Also the children were often ill with infectious diseases such as whooping cough, scarletina or measles, causing up to half to be absent. Deaths were not unheard of, and when things got really serious, the Doctor of Health would come and order the school to be closed for a period of time.

1918

The school log makes interesting reading, particularly during the time of Mary Seward, who made some descriptive entries. We can see that she thought the pupils scruffy and unclean, and often sent them home for a wash. She also had her fair share of problems:

November 14th 1878   Several children punished this week for destroying the Laurel round the school.
To which she added: *Very wet, only 71 present.*
December 6th 1878   Elizabeth Gibbs, who has made four attendances this week, was stood out this morning and told to hold a slate over her head for punishment, having run out of school yesterday and told a lie saying her mother had called her. She refused to hold the slate over her head for which she was put in the lobby, when she immediately ran home.
March 25th 1879   Sent to Mrs Mayne to enquire where one of her children was born. She came to the school in a great passion saying that there was always something to enquire about and that she was tired of answering.
April 25th 1879   Henry Goddard and William Mayne are two very obstinate and insubordinate boys. Caned them both and threatened them with expulsion.

The log mostly comments about the standard of work and the quality of the teachers, but the summary for 1890 includes the following:

The offices want careful looking into. The system appears to be the dry cesspit with trap door requiring daily earth or ashes to be thrown in, besides which regular disinfectant should be used.
And also in 1890:   *............. but there are lewd inscriptions in the girls' offices attributed to the members of the Sunday School. Against such contamination the day school children should have been protected.*

1928

Attendance registers for 1923-1933 show 155 children were admitted, 32 of whom came from St Benet's Home. At various times it has been called Emmer Green National School, Emmer Green Church of England School, and St Barnabas School. It finally closed in 1933 due to lack of support. All local children then had to attend the schools in Caversham. The building was gutted by fire in 1977 and demolished a few months later (Unity Court now occupies the site).

PHOTO DONATED BY JOHN DARBY

Emmer Green Primary School

Pupils spent four years in a converted 270 year old tithe barn belonging to Caversham Grove, before a new purpose built school was opened next to the church along Grove Road. Emmer Green County Primary School was built by Mr H Russell of Woodley at a cost of £57,000, admitting 250 children on 15th September 1952. The school was divided into two, four infant and three junior classes, all under the headship of Miss Phyllis Bone. In November of that year a gale blew the roof off the junior toilets, but apart from that it appears the school quickly settled into a regular routine.

On May 11th 1953 the school was officially opened by Miss J Elliot, the head of Queen Anne's School in Caversham. She remarked that it was a charming building in a delightful setting, and had no doubt that the work would be sound and honest, with teachers and pupils taking a pride in everything they did. The Mayor of Reading, Cllr F H Lewis recalled his last visit had been when the site was a sea of mud, and the roof had yet to be constructed.

The founding ethos of the school was to give children a broad balanced curriculum and adapted to suit individual needs. The hope is to create a secure, happy, stimulating environment to make pupils not only self-reliant, but considerate for others and able to develop their full potential. The 1990s have seen the introduction of the National Curriculum, League Tables, and Ofsted inspections. These have always shown the school in a good light, with successive improvements over the years. By the time the children are eleven years old they are ready to move on. The school has close links with Highdown School, but some pupils opt for Chiltern Edge in Sonning Common, and a few pass to Reading's remaining grammar schools.

Mrs Melinda Gane

Mr Michael Doyle and Staff 1977

PHOTO DONATED BY SALLY TRINDER

PHOTO DONATED BY MELINDA GANE

PHOTO CLIVE ORMONDE

Mrs Hardcastle at the Christmas Fair

There have been four permanent heads during the life of the school, Miss Bone remaining there for 18 years. Her successor Mrs Hodgsom remained until 1976, to be followed by Michael Doyle. Mrs Melinda Gane took over in 1987. It was during the headship of Miss Bone that school numbers soared, requiring additional temporary classrooms to be added to accommodate the extra children. This has been the trend again in the 1990s, and a permanent extension to the school opened in 2002.

Records show that in 1967 the school had its first television. As the years progressed the parents have increasingly contributed toward the school, by giving both time and money. The continued fundraising of the PTFA has contributed to many activities and provided vital equipment. The Christmas Fair is one of the high spots of the year, but other fund-raising events include sponsored reads, jumble sales and craft fairs. The Tesco voucher scheme suplements the school's stock of computers. Volunteers listen to the children read, or help with after school activities, such as the cycling proficiency courses. For a long while Lady Durant was Chairman of the Governors, and worked hard alongside staff to ensure the smooth running of the school.

Sponsored Bounce 1988

PHOTO E G SCHOOL

54

Emmer Green School Cricket Team 1957

Emmer Green School Football Team 1959

Sport has always been strong at the school, both for team and individual competition.

Miss Bone was keen that all children should learn to swim, and together with the help of the parents, plans were made to build a pool. In 1958 a fête was held in aid of the swimming pool fund, at which the pool was officially opened by 'champion swimmers from Reading Swimming Club'. The fete raised £150, completing the amount required to pay for the pool (£350 from the LEA and £507 from the school). It maintained a strong tradition of teaching swimming, and in 1965 the National Council of Women recognised it as the school with the most children learning to swim in the summer term. The pool served the school for many years, until by the mid 1990s the high cost of maintaining it for limited summer use led to a decision to fill it in, and create a quiet area. The school has extensive grounds and in one corner is a wildlife garden.

In 1954 the 1st XI football team won the Primary Schools Rufus Isaacs Shield for the first time, setting a strong tradition of football success for Emmer Green School. The photograph *(left)* shows the winners of the League and Cup football competitions for 1959/60

Music and drama are also important to the school. In addition to the resident music teacher, peripatetic specialists give lessons to small groups. The summer concerts follow a musical tradition, with both choral and instrumental work whilst the Christmas plays either re-enact the traditional nativity theme, or, for the older children, a pantomime story.

Dick Whittington 1970

Nativity Play 1989

The Hill School

A Class of the Late 1950s

A Class of the Mid 1980s

The school was built on seven acres of land, the former home of Caversham Cricket Club, overlooking Reading and the Thames Valley, at a cost of £70,000. The original name of The Hill School was changed to Caversham Park School in 1963, but had to revert to The Hill again when the new primary school opened on Caversham Park Village in 1970. Demand for places has always meant space has been at a premium for The Hill School. In fact when it opened on 18th September 1950 for over 300 children, only the classroom block was in use, with the remainder of the school under construction. On January 22nd 1952 the completed school was officially opened by Mr J F Wolfenden CBE, Vice Chancellor of Reading University. In September of the same year Emmer Green Primary School opened and sixty of the pupils transferred there. By the time Her Majesty's Inspectors visited the school in 1957, the pupil roll was at an all time peak of 425. It was noted by the inspectors that in spite of areas such as the dining hall, the vestibule and the small crush hall being used as classrooms, and many forms exceeding forty, the achievements of the school were very good, with tribute being paid to the headmistress Miss E M F Alderson.

Two of a total of six head teachers have served more than fifteen years at the school, the first being Miss Alderson who was at the helm when the school opened. It was during her headship in 1955 that the original swimming pool was built with funds being raised towards its £300 cost. Some fourteen years later soon after Miss Alderson's retirement, the Parents' Association was formed, and their first objective was to build a larger swimming pool. This pool was in use until the early 1990s when the high cost of maintenance and restricted use led to the decision to fill it in. Three successive heads followed Miss Alderson before Mr Alan Hyland joined the school in 1978. Under his guidance the school set about new ventures, such as the annual residential trips to Rhos-y-Gwaliau, South Wales. In 1983 he took the school into the IT age with the purchase of a BBC microcomputer. Progression in technology has meant that by the year 2000 every classroom was connected to the Internet. In 1997 Mr Wil Lambert was appointed to replace long serving head Alan Hyland.

Well loved caretaker Charlie Brown, retired in 1989 after thirty years' service at the school.

A full Ofsted inspection of the school in 1999 praised the quality of the teaching and caring relationships fostered in the school. Continued academic success ensures the pupils are well prepared for secondary education and beyond.

The Hill's proximity to the BBC Monitoring Station means that Russian is the most frequently spoken second language.

Mr R N Vandrill and Staff 1977

The school has always had a tradition of planting in its grounds to mark a particular occasion. Thirty-three trees marked the Coronation of Queen Elizabeth II, with another three to commemorate her Silver Jubilee in 1977. As part of the Millennium and its own fiftieth birthday celebrations daffodil bulbs were planted in the shape of a '50'. Mayor Bob Green planted a commemorative tree and helped the children bury a time capsule to be opened in the year 2050.

Each year children from both infant and junior schools were involved in dramatic, or musical performances. Christmas nativity plays were the tradition in the early years. During the 1980s it became the custom for the Year 6 to put on a musical farewell performance. With the help of other staff, teacher Mrs Ann Robinson produced these shows which included Joseph and his Multi-coloured Coat, Oklahoma, and an Old-fashioned Music Hall. Arts and crafts sessions were also popular, and parents often assisted small groups of enthusiastic children.

Sport in the early days included a game called shinty, a type of Scottish hockey. In March 1953 the school took part in a rally held at Brock Barracks, with other schools in the Reading area. The photograph on the left shows a cricket team in the 1950s. Football has always been practised and encouraged, and at one time training sessions were led by two stalwart fathers, Les Joyce and Bob Cox. As recently as 1994 the soccer team triumphed, being winners of the Schools' League Shield. The traditional school sports day is one of the highlights of the summer term.

PHOTOS HILL SCHOOL COLLECTION

The Grove Secondary/ Highdown School

When Reading Education Committee bought Caversham Grove in 1932, comprising the mansion and outbuildings set in 31 acres of land, its ultimate intention was to open it as a school. These ambitions however were not realised for another twenty years (see p 29) when The Grove Secondary School opened in September 1952 for local children from the ages of 11 upwards. By the time these once grand rooms in the mansion had more functional uses as classrooms, their original social purpose was just a fading memory. The dining room became the sixth form common room, whilst a bedroom might be a study or library. The 270 year old tithe barn which for several years had served the local primary school was the new assembly hall.

The official opening took place on 11th May 1953 (the same day as Emmer Green Primary School's), and was performed by the Rt Rev A G Parham, the Bishop of Reading, who declared, not only had a valuable education resourse been provided, but the fabric of one of England's country houses saved.

It was nearly another twenty years before another milestone passed, when it was transformed into Reading's biggest school, and its first comprehensive. It opened in September 1970, and was designed to house 1000 boys and girls , mostly from its predecessor The Grove Secondary School, and from E P Collier Central School in Caversham. Highdown School, as it became known, still used the older premises of Caversham Grove mansion for part of its space, but most of the accommodation was purpose built.

Staff at The Grove Secondary School 1963

It was divided into nine faculties to cover a wide range of teaching for pupils aged 11-18 years. The school was divided into Lower School, Middle School and Upper School with the emphasis on a broad curriculum. The head presiding over this change at the time was Mr R Brooker, and he viewed the future with great excitement. New facilities included a fine library, purpose built science block, excellent lecture theatre, good swimming pool and gymnasium, and piped television linking the classrooms. The tithe barn (below) was transformed into a music room.

PHOTOS HIGHDOWN COLLECTION

The most dramatic change since the early days has been the advance in technology. In 1993 the school was awarded £190,000 under the Government's Technology Schools Initiative. This was to be just the start of ensuring greater pupil access to computers, and several partnerships and initiatives have ensured this. One example was in 1996 when the school set up a leading edge superhighways trial, the Highdown Information Hub, in conjunction with Microsoft, ICL and Telecential. Such enterprises are ongoing to maintain the impact of new technology.

As well as academic, technological, sporting and creative opportunities, pupils are encouraged to use their skills and talents to serve the local community. An example of this was 'Green Week' organised in conjunction with Reading Borough Council, for Year 9 pupils in 1993 to raise environmental awareness. The event was launched by Reading's mayor, Cllr Rajinder Sohpal (photo right), and as well as on-site projects, the pupils explored Clayfield Copse nature reserve and visited Emmer Green pond.

Children of all abilities have the opportunity to participate in a wide choice of sports, either in lessons, or at after-school clubs. Sports teams regularly compete against other local schools. The school's excellent sporting facilities were formally opened to the wider community, when in the early 1990s a partnership was formed with Reading Leisure Services. The arrangement also brings in valuable income for the school. Other uses are made of the premises outside school hours. Reading Adult College provides further education courses, whilst in the summer holidays the school becomes host to foreign language students, and local children's activity weeks.

The school's income is further enhanced by the work of the Parent Teachers' Association. They hold events throughout the year, but the main attraction is the annual Highdown Show (photo right), held in the spring. This attracts folk from all over Reading, and is a tribute to the stalwart team of volunteers organising it. Financial contibutions have helped supply and support the school mini-bus, as well as a range of other projects.

Highdown's longest serving head was Andrew Clarke who was appointed in 1975 and remained in his post for nearly twenty years. Mr Tim Royle leads the school into the 21st century aided by over sixty dedicated teaching staff, plus a team of administrative and support personnel.

Health

Emmer Green residents today take for granted the fine facilities and care they receive from the surgery at 4 St Barnabas Road. It is thanks to the dedication and commitment of its predecessors that such a valuable asset exists today.

Some fifty years ago Dr Ian Clarke lived at 19 St Barnabas Road and ran a small surgery from that house. Unfortunately he fell ill with serious kidney problems, and despite being the first recipient of a kidney transplant (donated by his colleague Dr David Spencer), he died in 1962, and there was no longer a resident GP in Emmer Green. Although there were doctors' surgeries in Caversham, the parent surgery for Emmer Green was in Castle Street, Reading. A succession of doctors was employed from there to make home visits, but it wasn't until Dr Adamson was appointed to care specifically for the Emmer Green area, that things settled down. By now 19 St Barnabas Road had been sold, and a base for a new surgery was sought.

In early 1964 the Goodworth family moved into 14 St Barnabas Road, and offered temporary accommodation in a spare part of their house. This change of circumstance brought a rush of new patients, and Dr Adamson was obliged to open his surgery every afternoon. Very soon, he had to request help from the doctors in an Oxford Road practice to share night duties and help with the day surgeries. Things again reached crisis point later that year when Dr Adamson announced he was going to emigrate to Canada. The two most elderly doctors from the Oxford Road surgery, Dr Caiger-Smith and Dr Pirquet, asked if they could take over the practice until they retired. The Goodworths were faced with the difficult decision of whether to offer their rooms on a more permanent basis, but realised that unless they did so the local people would again be without a doctor. In fact, it is thanks to them, that this arrangement continued for the next 16 years.

Patient numbers continued to rise, creating the need for both administrative and nursing staff. The workload on the two ageing doctors however was tremendous, giving them no time to look for new premises. After ten years the situation became desperate with several thousand patients registered, and no solution in sight. Help arrived at last in the shape of Dr John McNie, son-in-law of Dr Caiger-Smith. As well as relieving the two older doctors of some of their surgeries, he was also allowed to see some of his patients in Emmer Green Clinic. He took on the task of reorganising the surgery and looking for a new site.

This proved a most onerous undertaking. Land on the site of the old Emmer Green School was deemed ideal, and plans drawn up, but the Council insisted it was required for housing. Use of any suitable existing property was opposed by local residents fearful of the potential traffic congestion. A site off the Kiln Road had to be abandoned because of legal entanglements. Finally, as the long overdue retirement of Drs Caiger-Smith and Pirquet approached, persistence paid off. Dr McNie spotted a wide grass verge alongside a service road behind St Barnabas Church. The Council approved, the land was purchased, and the original plans adapted for the site. The operation moved ahead swiftly and the new surgery opened at the end of 1980. The three doctors finally achieved what they desired and retirement for the two older ones was now possible. Sadly they both died within the next year.

PHOTO CLIVE ORMONDE

During the twenty years since the **Emmer Green Surgery** opened it has gone from strength to strength. Several extensions have been added over the years and it now has consulting rooms for six doctors, treatment rooms for nurses and support staff, as well as room for office staff, and a fully computerised system. Health visitors are also now based at the surgery, as is the **Emmer Green Clinic**, which for many years had its own building in Grove Road to serve mothers, babies and children. The future of the health and welfare of the patients is at last secure.

Heathcroft in Marshlands Square, home for youngsters with special needs was also innovative when it was built in 1976. After twenty five years of service it is moving to more suitable premises on the other side of Reading. Its aim was to offer respite care and help parents cope with looking after their child. There was a structured programme to help the children build life skills and integrate into the community. The hostel catered for up to 150 children up to the age of nineteen, most of whom attended for one or two sessions a week. It also had a longstay unit for a handful of children. Also, just off Marshlands Square is the **St Luke's Court**, which caters for the needs of the elderly, either by offering sheltered independent housing or residential/nursing care. It was built in the grounds of Springfield St Luke House in the late 1980s, followed by adjacent home, **The Oaks,** in the late 1990s.

Law and Order

PC Jack Parker in the 1930s

Long gone are the days when everyone knew the village 'bobby' and his presence ensured things never got out of hand. PC Jack Parker lived in Emmer Green most of his life. Jack was well loved and respected by all. He kept ferrets and would happily lend one to anyone wanting to go rabbiting. He was big in stature, and wasn't above giving a clip round the ear to any youngster caught scrumping! He was due to retire in the late 1930s, but war broke out and he was kept on. These were the days when children had freedom to explore the countryside unsupervised, but any of a mischevious nature were severely dealt with. An event is recalled of how a couple of lads broke into the greenkeeper's hut in Cucumber Wood to shelter from a storm. They thought they would practise golf with the balls they discovered.....the result was they appeared before the Henley Magistrates and were given two years probation. A police box was situated opposite the pond before the brick building appeared on Marshlands Square.

It was in the late 1960s when another highly regarded policeman arrived on the scene in the shape of PC Jim Titcombe. He was appointed under the new 'village policeman' scheme, and Jim wasted no time in getting to know the district and the people under his care. He became a familiar cheery figure as he patrolled the streets on his motor-cycle and had an amazing capacity for remembering everyone he met. His work in schools and youth clubs gave youngsters a new sense of security, and encouraged them to grow up with a positive attitude towards the police. Sadly, after five years of serving the community PC Titcombe collapsed and died suddenly at his home in 1973. After his death residents raised money to give to his family, and the Council provided a seat near the children's play area in Caversham Park, where a plaque pays tribute to him. Both his daughter, Annette, and her husband PC Small followed in his footsteps and patrolled Emmer Green in the 1980s.

PC Jim Titcombe visits The Hill School

In the 1990s it was PC Phill Webster (*pictured right*) who was to becomet a familiar figure around Emmer Green. He joined the police after a long army career and lived locally with his family. He was happy to be known locally as 'Phill the Fuzz', and was frequently seen off duty walking his rotweiller dog Rocky and carrying his radio to monitor events. One of Rocky's biggest challenges came when he was electrocuted as a result of relieving himself on a damaged lamppost. Undeterred, the dog resumed his duties after a brief period of recuperation. PC Webster was one of the first in the area to patrol through the night.

We are lucky to live in a relatively crime free area, but it seems an anomaly that when the population has grown so much policing on the ground has not kept pace. Neighbourhood Watch schemes have been introduced as a self-help measure, but this does not prevent or discourage petty crime or wanton vandalism.

Shops

In 1881 Edward Allnutt was recorded as a baker and grocer, and lived on the premises with his wife and three young children. Ten years later the village grocery had been taken over by a widower, Mr Taylor. At least three of his five children helped in the store. In the early 1900s a butcher's shop was run by a Mr Kirkpatrick who operated from a lock-up shed in the front garden of one of the cottages on the corner of the Kidmore End and Peppard Roads, near the smithy. On the corner of Fisher's Row was a small sweet and confectionery shop (*photo right*) run by Mrs Stratford. The main bakery (*photo below*) was on one side of The Black Horse and the granary on the other (18a Kidmore End Road). The grain was stored on the upper floor and the entrance for the horse and cart was underneath. There were also stables at the back of the bakery,

The Granary

PHOTO FISHER COLLECTION

with access from the pub yard. The ovens at the back of the shop remained long after baking ceased. In the 1920s it was run by Howard's of Caversham, and bread and delicious fancy cakes would be delivered daily. They also ran the Post Office. In the late 1930s the Pitticks lived above the shop and Mrs Pittick ran the Post Office. This shop was known to locals as the 'top shop', and when Howards gave up the Post Office side it moved across the road to the 'bottom shop' called Rice's, located in the front room of a row of cottages behind the smithy. The former smithy was then converted to a drapers and general store by the Fisher's firm. During the 1930s a muffin man sold his wares from a stall in Kidmore End Road. By the 1960s the Howard's bakery had become a butcher's shop (*photo right*), one of several in the area belonging to the Jennings family. A variety of uses followed until in the 1990s it opened up as a Tandoori restaurant.

Howard's Bakery and Post Office in the 1920s

READING LIBRARY SERVICES

The first garage and filling station, run by Ern Johnson, was built on the western side of the Peppard Road, and it had one petrol pump with a long arm overhanging the road. It was in 1936 that another garage was built directly opposite by S Iven & Son for Frank Bevan and his partner Mr Bastin. The drawing of architect J H Willett showed it as The Park Motor Company Ltd ,but it is doubted if it was ever called that. When war broke out and petrol shortages bit, business suffered. The garage forecourt was dug up to grow vegetables! In the mid 1950s the garage was bought by international rally drivers Samuel Moore and Douglas Johns. They ran an agricultural services company, and it was only later that it resumed its original function as the **Emmer Green Garage**. In October 1983 a spectacular fire destroyed most of the building, to the distress of Mr Moore. The very next day his workers returned to begin preparing for work. It was rebuilt and continued to undertake car & petrol sales and mechanical repairs. The petrol sales side of the business ceased in 1998.

PHOTO DONATED BY SAMUEL MOORE

Peter Jennings serving in his Shop

Eventually the old smithy and some nearby cottages were demolished and the present shops built. Bob Hodges (real character and noted rugby player) ran the Post Office and established a thriving general store. A dragon originally made at the brickworks for the forge stood over the shop. Next to Hodges' shop was a hairdressers run by Dougie Hutchings, son of the landlord of the Black Horse. The real change came in 1970 when the shopping precinct was built as part of the Caversham Park development. The complex comprised a major supermarket (Budgens), as well as a number of smaller shops which have served the community well over the years. Unfortunately this was to have a serious impact on Mr Hodges' trade, and eventually his shop was sold to the Balfour chain of newsagents. Before the shopping precinct was built Caversham was the nearest main centre. Mobile shops were a boon, however. A van based in Grove Road toured with groceries; Jennings, the butcher came round with meat; and the Co-op called on a Monday to take orders which were delivered the following Friday. Home deliveries today are undergoing something of a revival thanks to the Internet. Milk deliveries began many years ago when local dairy farmers would visit the neighbourhood with milk churns. Today the traditional milkfloat has to compete with the supermarkets. There are still a couple of regular traders who pitch their stalls near the shops to sell fresh fish or flowers.

Public Houses

The three public houses currently operating in Emmer Green have a very long history, although only one, The White Horse, remains in its original location. They were all situated on main routes out of Reading and offered stabling for horses and either a cart house or a coach house.

At one time there was a fourth inn called **The Grove Arms**. Its precise location is unknown, but it is believed to be in the vicinity of Grove Farm. The 1881 census shows the occupant to be Thomas Parker. The following year a licence was granted to Henry Filbee to sell retail beer to be consumed 'off' the premises. However in October 1882 he was convicted, fined and imprisoned for opening his house during prohibited hours, and for allowing drinking 'on' the premises. In 1883 his licence was opposed and refused.

PHOTO FISHER COLLECTION

Mr & Mrs Birch and Spot the Dog host the celebration of the Coronation of Edward VII 1902

The White Horse inn on Kidmore End Road, has always been at the centre of village life. Records suggest an inn has stood on the site since the 16th century. Situated beside a main northerly route out of Reading, it served as place of refreshment to travellers and locals alike. Its early history as a coaching inn is speculation, but outwardly the building has changed very little. The adjacent smithy and outside stabling remained until the early part of the 20th century. Throughout the 1800s the blacksmith was also the publican and beerseller, at a time when it was common for the licensee to have other interests. It was owned by Simonds, the Reading brewers, and the original licence was for beer to be consumed 'on' the premises. From the early 1880s until 1907 there were a number of innkeepers often lasting no longer than a couple of years. It was William Bunch who offered stability from 1907-1923. Ernest Mortimer (*below*) was the innkeeper 1923-1951, and he and his family played an important part in the community, supporting both

The White Horse in the 1930s

PHOTO FISHER COLLECTION

football and rugby teams by offering changing facilities at the pub. One of his successors, Frank Clayson continued this tradition, donating a silver cup for the football charity matches (see p95). By 1936 a wine licence had been granted, but it wasn't until nearly twenty years later that the beerhouse licence was surrendered for a full publican's licence.

PHOTO DONATED BY GEOFFREY MORTIMER

There were few restrictions in the early years and local farmers would slip in to the White Horse for their early morning ale, whilst waiting for their horses to be shod next door. There are even rumours of one regular who drank eighteen pints of beer, seven days a week, and still lived to a ripe old age! Before the Second World War there was a core of regular customers, many of them living on the doorstep, but some used to come from Caversham and Binfield Heath. Whilst preserving its role as the focus of everyday village life, the inn has also played host to some notable people. D R Jardine, captain of the England cricket team that toured Australia in 1932/3 (noted for the bodyline controversy) was a customer. American heavyweight Boxing Champion Joe Louis used to call in at the pub on his way to the golf course, when he was stationed locally during the war years 1942/3. Other celebrities included Gilbert Harding the broadcaster, and Geoffrey Grigson the naturalist. A Russian prince who was stationed at the BBC, André Belososki, was remembered for his magnificent singing voice!

Interior of The White Horse 1975   PHOTO FISHER COLLECTION

Food and lodging were always available at the inn, with guests sleeping in an open dormitory, but the inn had no bathroom until the 1950s. Internal renovations have taken place at intervals over the years. Until 1973 the inn comprised a number of small rooms - one for cribbage; one for darts (the team were winners of the Reading Trophy in 1938); one for skittles, and another for singing and the gossip of the day. There is an early history of bread baking at the inn, and right up until the 1920s it sold groceries, as well as beer. People often took their Sunday dinners to the pub to be cooked in the bakehouse ovens. granted. In 1973 a dining area was added, and internal walls knocked down to give open plan facilities. The beams were exposed, and a number of the remaining artefacts were put on display. Further restructuring ten years later saw the main entrance move from the main building to a side annexe. In 1993 the then owners provoked fierce local opposition when they changed the name to the 'Pickled Newt'! Fortunately it quickly reverted back to The White Horse. The pub was closed for a couple of months in early 1998, and again late in 2002, whilst the brewers Greene King undertook comprehensive refurbishment. It was at this time that Pond House, immediately behind the inn and for many years home of the Bew family, was transformed into the kitchen area of the pub. The sign hanging outside has also seen changes, and it was a regular customer in the 1950s who suggested a design based on the British Gold Slater coin unearthed near St Barnabas Church (see p23). The sign depicted a warrior mounted on a white horse.

The White Horse 1975

PHOTO FISHER COLLECTION

Opposite The White Horse is **The Black Horse**. This was originally situated on the old Peppard Road, next to the Chapel-on-the-Hill. It is not known precisely when it was moved, but the reasons for the transfer are related on page 72. Thomas Fewster was one of the last recorded landlords on the original site. By 1852 he had been succeeded by Ephraim Grant, victualler, coal merchant and cattle dealer. Jesse Kirkpatrick served from at least 1877 -1891 by which time it was clearly in its present location. The Heather family who were already living in nearby cottages took over in 1892 and remained until 1912. One of their cottages is still occupied by a relative, John Darby and their great-grandson, Adrian Darby, still lives in Emmer Green. The local fire brigade used to keep their fire cart in the Black Horse Yard, and the pegs where the firemen used to hang their coats remain to this day. There was great excitement in the village when the firemen were called out, and they would be waved on their way by a crowd of onlookers. Horace Hutchings was publican for a long time from 1933 onwards and it was during the post-war period that jolly Saturday nights were held with live bands and dancing to the music. The Black Horse has always had a full licence enabling it to sell spirits as well as beer and wine.

The Black Horse circa 1910

Some way from these two pubs is **The Gardeners' Arms**, or 'The Old Ale House' as it was once known. Both old and new versions of the inn are in Surley Row, and unlike the original Black Horse, the first Gardeners' Arms still stands as house No 46 (see p 32). The 1844 tithe map shows the public house beside an orchard and the occupant as Charles Fuller. James Harrison who held a beer licence from 1883-1900 was described as a publican and market gardener. There followed a number of licensees until in 1914 George Cox took over, to be succeeded by his daughter ten years later. The licence was temporarily revoked in1925, when the pub was rebuilt in the adjoining orchard. Miss Cox handed over to James Smith, but remained in the house until the 1970s. The new 'Gardeners' Arms was fully operational by 1927, and since then has acquired a history of its own. A special feature is the skittle alley, purpose built at the rear of the premises.

The Gardeners' Arms circa 1960

Roads

Knights Way 1949

Until the early part of the twentieth century road tarring was unknown, and many roads were a sea of mud during the winter months. Large quantities of flints were picked off the fields and placed in piles by the side of roads or tracks for road making. It was common to see men breaking large flints from the heaps at the roadside.

Many early routes through from Reading to South Oxfordshire passed through Emmer Green. Surley Row is a very ancient highway leading on to Highdown Hill Road and cutting across what is now the golf course. No longer a through route, the track at the northern end has recently been promoted to Sustrans Cycleway No 5. Grove Hill is also a very old route, the top half linking it to Surley Row is now just a footpath. The Peppard Road, until the mid-nineteenth century called the Nettlebed Road, has undergone considerable change. On at least two occasions road widening was considered. The first, in the late 1930s, involved the demolition of an historic Tudor cottage, opposite Blenheim House (see p38), but war intervened and the widening never took place. Another controversy occurred nearly forty years later when it was found the building of the new shopping precinct obstructed a line of prospective road improvement. As construction was well underway it was allowed to continue, and again the road widening never materialised. Between these two considerations there was one major change, and this was executed in conjunction with the building of the council housing estate in 1949. Buckingham Drive effectively created a new main road through Emmer Green, turning a long stretch of the original Peppard Road into a quiet lane. It also meant the removal of a small pond next to the main pond.

Peppard Road in the 1930s

Road names are often not arbitrary, they have historical connections. Some relate to a former use of the land, such as Spinney Close, School Lane, Kiln Road and Sheep Walk, whilst others like Gravel Hill, or Highdown ('hay hill') Hill Road have geological and agricultural origins, respectively. Grove Hill, Grove Road, and Rosehill Park, relate to estates of the same name, whilst Crawshay Drive commemorates the 19th century Welsh ironmaster. Eric Avenue is named after the son of the builder, Jack Bridges.

Peppard Road in the Year 2000

Transport

Before the days of mass organised transport, most workmen walked to work, even journeys up to ten miles. For a long time, for many people in Emmer Green, the only way to get to Caversham or Reading was to walk down the old Peppard Road. People were able to organise their own transport for various excursions, both local and further afield. There were Sunday outings to the cherry orchards of Stoke Row by horse and carriage (photo above), to picnic in the countryside and pick or buy cherries. A more adventurous trip was organised by PC Jack Parker in 1920s. It was a day trip to Southsea by charabanc (photo left). Unfortunately as it could only do twelve miles an hour, most of the day was spent travelling.

The outlying villages of Reading depended on the carrier's van to get into town and the first, operated by House Bros of Watlington, can be traced back to 1912. Petrol shortages during World War I slowed progress down, but after it ended the Thames Valley Traction Company ran route No 7 through Emmer Green to Nettlebed. Later Bill Jackman from Stoke Row ran the first combined carrier and passenger service. Sam Hall ran his from Checkendon. The 1930 Traffic Act meant a lot of paper work for the small operators and Jackman and Hall were taken over by Harry Kemp, the fore-runner of the Chiltern Queens.

Gyclists Ern and Bob Short and Harry Pittick

Mrs Matilda Watts of Westfield Road, Caversham ran the first motorised bus service from Reading to Peppard via Emmer Green and Kidmore End. The plum red coloured bus was called the 'Rapide' and the fare from Reading to Emmer Green was 4d.

The first Corporation bus service commenced in May 1925 and ran from Emmer Green to Lower Whitley. The bus was a Guy single decker No11and for reasons of safety it terminated at the junction of Grove Road and Kidmore End Road. The terminus was extended to Chalgrove Way in the early 1930s, at the same time as double

No 23 'Standee' Bus in 1968

deckers were introduced. During World War II, to confuse the enemy, the destination board was actually changed from Emmer Green to 'Chalgrove Way'. Even one local serviceman returning from war duties had to ask where the Emmer Green bus was. Mr Charles Kelsey, who has lived in Emmer Green for most of his life, worked for Reading Corporation in 1946 and drove buses from Lower Whitley (The Grenadier) to Chalgrove Way. His route stopped at Noble's Way or Hill, at the junction of Surley Row and Peppard Road, before continuing along what is now the old Peppard Road. After stopping at the BBC it would then cross straight into Kidmore End Road (no Buckingham Drive). Mr Kelsey remembers well, having to back into Chalgrove Way, the terminus, before making the return journey. By the 1950s alternate buses went as far as Courtenay Drive. This progressed into a combination of the 24 and the 23, which completed the circuit in the opposite direction. It's rumoured that passengers walking from Highdown Hill Avenue across the golf course on wet days would leave their 'wellies' under the seat at the bus stop, and collect them on their return from town. Unfortunately moans about the service are nothing new, and when many houses were built in the late forties and early fifties, there was a tirade of complaints about various inadequacies.

The early buses which ran from 1935-1950 were low-bridge buses, or "head-bumpers". There was an open doorway at the back, seats for four, and a gangway down one side on the upper deck. The single decker 'standee' buses introduced in the late 1960s were the fore-runners of the current double-deckers.

Bicycles would have no doubt helped many people get around, and perhaps in the 1930s some of the better off folk owned cars. It was after the war that car ownership really took off, and escalated to the degree that by the turn of the twentieth century there were often two or three per household.

Cars now dominate Emmer Green for personal transport, but the freedom and independence that people treasure comes at a price. Roads become more and more congested and car-parking impossible. The value of a regular, efficient bus service becomes more apparent.

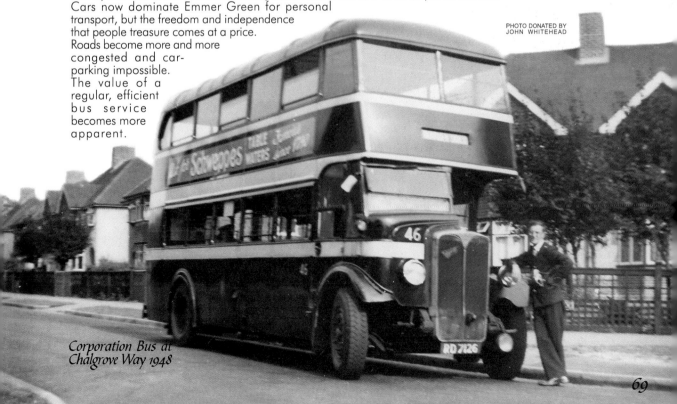

Corporation Bus at Chalgrove Way 1948

Community Buildings

As the village population grew, so the need for a meeting place, or hall transpired. A distinctive **'Iron Room'** *(photo right)* was brought up from the Forbury Gardens in the 1870s and erected in Kidmore End Road, on land opposite the common. Its initial use was as a parish room. Mrs Foster-Brown, who later lived at Caversham Grove, ran a Mothers' Meeting in the tin hut. All married women were welcome, and those who were childless were obliged to borrow a child to qualify for membership! It was also hired out for wedding receptions and parties, but the local scout group was able to use it free of charge. It remained a landmark in Emmer Green until the 1980s when it was demolished.

PHOTO HIGHDOWN COLLECTION

Mr Sutton who lived at Kidmore Grange (Rosehill House) owned a public hall in Kidmore End Road (opposite the entrance to St Benet's Home). The hall was used for concerts, lectures, and religious services. It was demolished at the end of the First World War, and houses were built on the site.

PHOTO CLIVE ORMONDE

St Barnabas Church Hall began life as the church itself *(see page 46)*. It was at a meeting held in October 1926, that the Rector of Caversham set up a committee to run the former church in Grove Road as a hall, for the benefit of the community. An application for a dancing and music licence was quickly granted, but no dancing whatsoever was to be allowed on Saturday evenings. This was followed by the purchase of a piano for 39 guineas. In the early years fortunes fluctuated, but by 1938 it was advertised as "Hall has up-to-date dressing and retiring rooms, is lighted throughout with electric light, including footlights to spacious stage, is suitable for whist drives, dances and meetings". During and immediately after the war, the hall functioned as a school *(see page 51)*. The Emmer Green Social Club which flourished throughout the fifties was based at the hall. Many other groups sprang up in the 1950s and early 60s *(see chapter on Sport and Recreation),* often chosing the church hall as their starting base. Photographs taken during that time still show the original church windows. It has continued to provide good service ever since, not just for church related meetings and club venues, but regular jumble sales, fayres and private functions. It has been recognised for a while that the structure of the building is in need of replacement and in 1999 a fund was set up to raise money for this.

Emmer Green **Youth and Community Centre** was purpose built in 1969. It was part of the extensive development of the youth service nationally, and locally, as recommended by the Albemarle Report. Facilities included a hall, stage and bar areas, and a team of full time youth workers and volunteers helped run the various organisations set up *(see page 101)*. Many of those who began their careers at the Youth Centre went on to make important contributions to youth work in Reading and Berkshire. Detta Ochanski (later Regan), the youth worker in the 1980s, was awarded European Woman of the Year 2001 for her work on the international stage. Although the focus is still on youth, the centre actually caters for a very wide age group. The Toddler Group caters for children under three, and the Pre-school Playgroup moved there from St Barnabas Hall in the late 1980s. There have also been successful after-school clubs, run for the children of Emmer Green Primary School. North Reading Youth Project provides social and educational opportunities for young people in a safe environment. There are two clubs for the over fifties.Other recreational and sports clubs meet there, and on Sundays it is the home of Caversham Evangelical Church.

PHOTO CLIVE ORMONDE

People

PHOTO: HARRIS FAMILY

PHOTO FISHER COLLECTION

PHOTO HILL SCHOOL COLLECTION   PHOTO DEBORAH WOOD

The Gentry

Right up until the early part of the twentieth century the big houses in and around Emmer Green were owned by individual families, often wealthy industrialists or bankers, who led lavish lifestyles. The social structures at that time were very clear, and the workers knew their place (see p88), but that did not mean the two could not enjoy a good relationship, and the examples here show what generous benefactors the masters were, and the respect and affection local people had for them.

The last family to live in Caversham Park were the Crawshays. William Crawshay owned the Cyfarthfa Ironworks in Merthyr Tydfil, South Wales, once the largest in the world. He bought the Caversham Park estate in 1844, and, when ten years later it was gutted by fire, he paid out of his own money to have it rebuilt around an iron frame. The building of the Great Western Railway meant that he could commute easily from Reading to Wales. In fact his return to Reading was welcomed by the locals, as it meant employment for them and more money to spend on ale. He was a religious man, however, and the sight of locals rushing from the Chapel to the adjacent Black Horse Inn led to the pub being relocated. He died in 1867 leaving £2 million, and his wife Isabella, who was remembered for her great kindness, remained in the house. As their son Robert died before his mother, the estate then passed to her grandson and his wife, Rose. W T Crawshay was the first President of the golf club. He died in 1918 and the estate passed to his nephew, Jack, who was remembered for riding around Emmer Green on a motorbike.

Frederick George Saunders owned and lived in Caversham Grove (see p29) from 1870 until his death aged eighty in 1901. He had no children, but his widow Elizabeth remained in the house until her death thirteen years later. The son of Robert Saunders of Kent, he followed in his uncle's footsteps to become Secretary of the Great Western Railway (1863-1886). He was much respected in railway circles and was elected Chairman in 1889, a post he held for six years. A man of some standing, he was an Oxford magistrate and honorary member of the Ancient Order of Foresters, the Emmer Green Court (Saunders Court) being named after him. He was an ardent Conservative and member of the Board of Management of the National Schools at Caversham. He was particularly remembered in Emmer Green as a generous friend to the poor and benefactor to local institutions and was of a genial and kindly disposition. When Mr Saunders returned from the Boer War his coachman met him at the station, and when his brougham reached Emmer Green all the male residents were lined up across the road. They unhitched the horses and pulled the brougham by the shafts, triumphantly home. He helped finance the building of the original St Barnabas Church and was a regular worshipper there. The church was specially carpeted and decorated with flowers for his funeral, which must have been a memorable event in Emmer Green. The hearse was followed by a procession of 33 carriages transporting family members, national and local dignitaries. Those gathered at the church to pay their respects also included local tradesmen and staff from Caversham Grove. As the funeral procession moved through Emmer Green towards St Peter's Church for internment residents closed blinds and shutters as a mark of respect. Mrs Saunders (right) continued to support the church, and would be pushed there every Sunday in her wheelchair by the young Laurie Hunt who was paid half a crown.

PHOTOS HIGHDOWN COLLECTION

Mr Richard Hatt Noble (left), who lived in Hill House, Surley Row (see p34), was referred to in 'Who's Who' as a 'gentleman'. For a number of years he shared a villa in Portugal with his brother Charles. Richard never married, but in time it was Charles' daughter, Emma, who came to keep house for her uncle, remaining there after his death. During his working life he was a director of Cox's Bank in London. He travelled from the house in a dog cart drawn by an enormous grey horse. The train at the Great Western station would be held up for his arrival, and because he travelled with large amounts of money about his person he had to be locked into a first-class carriage. Mr Noble was always thoughtful and generous to those who had helped him, and such gestures as taking spring violets from the estate as a gift for the wife of the bank's commissionaire were appreciated. In old age he was crippled and stone deaf, but the children of his staff gave him much pleasure and they would be rewarded with gifts or sovereigns. Miss Noble continued in this vein after her uncle died, 'adopting' an orphan, and taking an interest in the local school and St Benet's Home. She paid for the education of the sons of her employees, but the girls were not forgotten, and she was happy to set them up to go into service or prepare for motherhood.

The Fisher Family

PHOTO FISHER COLLECTION

The Business

The Fisher family moved to Emmer Green from Mapledurham in the 1880s and played a significant rôle in village life for over a century. William Fisher set up as a wheelwright and timber merchant on the Peppard Road, and in due course was joined by sons Noah and Edwin. **W N & E Fisher** had their own forge (see p86), and Edwin was the blacksmith. They also set up the family run, Belle Vue Hand Laundry (see page 89) in the Kidmore End Road.

Emmer Green village, being in the middle of a wholly agricultural area and on the road from South Oxfordshire to Reading, provided William with plenty of trade. William obtained his timber from the woods north of the village, particularly around Checkendon. He would ride out, select the trees he wanted to buy, have them felled then transported on a long cart pulled by a team of horses to his yard for cutting up by hand. With plenty of good local timber available, and as the business grew, carpentry was added to the trades advertised by the firm. Coffin making also became profitable and they were able to establish themselves as Undertakers and Funeral Directors. When a local death occurred the deceased person was removed to the mortuary of Messrs Ball in the Wokingham Road. A hearse was then hired from Messrs Lovegroves and a team of men from the yard would don black suits and act as pallbearers. Funerals from Springfield St Lukes (by this time a home for elderly ladies) were quite frequent, and undertaken for £60, with the pallbearers receiving 7/6d each.

In 1914, the year his father William died, George Russell Fisher and his wife Isabella moved from Sonning Common to live in Grove Place, Peppard Road, adjacent to the Fisher yard. This was the time he joined the firm, leaving Huntley & Palmers and bringing his building talents with him. As the motor car developed in the 1920s and 1930s causing a decline in the wheelwright and shoeing trade, George Russell was able to gradually change the business into a building firm. George and Isabella had six children, and the four sons brought with them a variety of talents. George William was a carpenter and joiner; Eric, a designer and architect; William Henry, a bricklayer; and Roy, the firms driver and decorator. An uncle, Walter George, set up as a qualified plumber and gas fitter. In the 1920s W N & E Fisher were building houses on the Grove Road and Peppard Road in Emmer Green and in Caversham, and in September 1924 the foundation stone of the new St Barnabas Church was laid. It was completed and consecrated on 28th June 1929. The firm also helped with the housing estate built after the war on Evesham Road and adjoining roads.

In 1937 George Russell bought his brother Edwin out of the firm, and ran it with his four sons until his death in 1959. Things were never quite the same without the driving force of George, but his sons continued until 1981, when eventually age crept up on the four brothers. At a directors' meeting they decided to sell the business to a Mr Harvey from Staines. It struggled along for few years, but with the Fisher family's interest declining, the site was finally sold in 1988 to Rockfort Development, and retirement flats (Fisher's Court) were built on the land. Only a building adjacent to the old forge remains and it is now a listed building.

The Family

William and his large family lived in Oak Villa, a detached house (241 Peppard Road), and several cottages (Grove Place) were built nearby for family members. They also owned much of the land behind the yard, and it was William who opened up Fisher's Row off Kidmore End Road to make a back entrance to his house. The Fisher family played a very active part in both church and community life. William Noah Fisher sang in the choir for 40 years. On a Saturday evening the Fisher children would read the collect, epistle and gospel, just in case they were chosen to read at church the next day.

George Russell Fisher taught the boys at The Oratory School woodwork. He also organised Saturday night dances, aided by Mrs Bell, to raise funds for the Red Cross. He was a good sportsman, playing for both the Emmer Green cricket and football teams.

The two Fisher girls, Phyllis and Esmé, did not join the family firm. Esmé married Norman Ellingham in 1940 and spent a great deal of her married life with her husband in East Africa. For his services to that country Norman was awarded the OBE. Phyllis did not marry and had several jobs as a typist, nurse and helping at the Belle Vue Hand Laundry. She was the girl in the family who traditionally stayed at home to look after parents. Phyllis was a great supporter of St Barnabas Church and was involved in all its activities. She played the piano for the Sunday School. During the war she was in the Red Cross, and later became a member of the Townswomen's Guild. Phyllis also put together a collection of many family and other photographs of Emmer Green which have become a fine historical record.

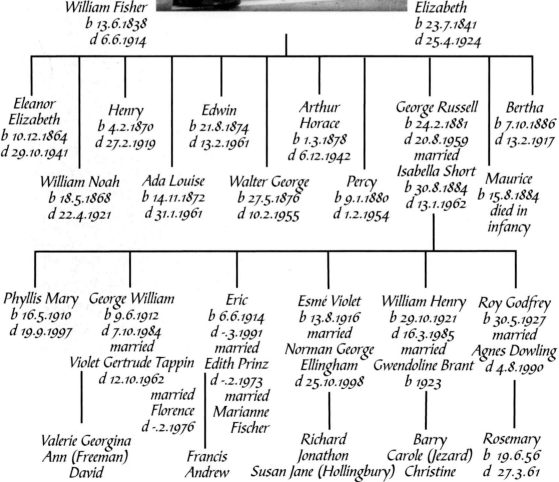

William Fisher
b 13.6.1838
d 6.6.1914

Elizabeth
b 23.7.1841
d 25.4.1924

Eleanor Elizabeth
b 10.12.1864
d 29.10.1941

Henry
b 4.2.1870
d 27.2.1919

Edwin
b 21.8.1874
d 13.2.1961

Arthur Horace
b 1.3.1878
d 6.12.1942

George Russell
b 24.2.1881
d 20.8.1959
married
Isabella Short
b 30.8.1884
d 13.1.1962

Bertha
b 7.10.1886
d 13.2.1917

William Noah
b 18.5.1868
d 22.4.1921

Ada Louise
b 14.11.1872
d 31.1.1961

Walter George
b 27.5.1876
d 10.2.1955

Percy
b 9.1.1880
d 1.2.1954

Maurice
b 15.8.1884
died in infancy

Phyllis Mary
b 16.5.1910
d 19.9.1997

George William
b 9.6.1912
d 7.10.1984
married
Violet Gertrude Tappin
d 12.10.1962
married
Florence
d -.2.1976

Eric
b 6.6.1914
d -.3.1991
married
Edith Prinz
d -.2.1973
married
Marianne Fischer

Esmé Violet
b 13.8.1916
married
Norman George Ellingham
d 25.10.1998

William Henry
b 29.10.1921
d 16.3.1985
married
Gwendoline Brant
b 1923

Roy Godfrey
b 30.5.1927
married
Agnes Dowling
d 4.8.1990

Valerie Georgina Ann (Freeman)
David

Francis
Andrew

Richard Jonathon
Susan Jane (Hollingbury)

Barry
Carole (Jezard)
Christine

Rosemary
b 19.6.56
d 27.3.61

The Mafeking Oak

A magnificent oak tree stood on the land of Park Farm, near the site of the present shopping precinct. It was felled on May 18th 1900, the date of the Relief of Mafeking, as a tribute to General Baden-Powell and his troops who had been defending the territory for seven months. One of Mr Fisher's men, Robert Briant, was a prisoner at Mafeking. The tree was transported to Fisher's yard on a long carriage pulled by a team of six fine horses. William Fisher was photographed standing by his great tree trunk lying on the cart, and the picture and an account were sent by William to General Baden-Powell. He received a reply from Mrs Baden-Powell thanking him and explaining that her son was still away. When he returned home at last from South Africa he wrote a letter of appreciation and enclosed a signed photo of himself.

THIS BRAVE OLD OAK FELL MAY 18th, 1900,
THE DATE OF THE RELIEF OF MAFEKING,
THE HEART OF OAK

The Ivens Family

By and large throughout the nineteenth and first half of the twentieth century Emmer Green still offered a traditional village life in a self-contained community. People tended to live their whole lives in houses where they were born, and inter-marriage within the village was common. They often had many children, some of whom followed in their footsteps, and successive generations took over skills and trades. There are still descendants of some of these people living in Emmer Green today, and the Ivens family are perhaps the best example, with four generations still living locally.

The Ivens Family at the Wedding of Ivy Ivens and Leslie May in 1929

The presence of the Ivens family in Kidmore End Road dates back at least to the 1870s. It was Alfred Ivens, born in 1847, the middle child of seven born to Stephen and Sarah Ivens of Caversham, who settled in one of the properties near the junction with the Peppard Road, with his wife Amelia and four children. Alfred was a bricklayer, and when he died it was Stephen his eldest child who supported his mother and remained with her in the house until he married Ellen Tilling in 1897. Alfred Ivens, Stephen's younger brother, eventually emigrated to Canada. Stephen and Ellen moved to a house further along Kidmore End Road where they were to raise ten children over a span of twenty years. When the house was deemed too small, Grandma Amelia came to the rescue by housing the two eldest boys.

Stephen Ivens became a skilled carpenter through his employment at G Lewis, Timber Merchants and Barge Builders of Caversham. His son Maurice joined him there in 1919. When it closed they both came to work for William Fisher, who by that time had already established his business in Emmer Green. Alfred, Stephen's eldest son, was employed by Serpells the biscuit makers, probably at their tin works in Liverpool Road. In 1925 Alfred Ivens secured a few plumbing jobs around Emmer Green village. The trade was such that the Fishers thought it might threaten their business and it became difficult for Stephen to remain in their employ. Eventually Stephen decided his future was with Alfred, and in1926/7 they set up S Ivens & Son, general builders. The Fishers wanted Maurice to remain in their employ, but he too left to join the burgeoning family firm. The business was situated on land beside the road leading to St Benet's Home, rented from Mrs Bell. As the remaining sons - Reg, Bert and Hugh - grew up they too helped run the family business. They brought with them building, carpentry and painting & decorating skills to compliment Alfred's plumbing. It was only William and Eric who sought different vocations. The 1920s was a good time for a building firm in Emmer Green and eventually the firm was to employ twenty people, taking their work well beyond the local area. It was S Ivens & Son who built the first Emmer Green Garage (*see page 62*).

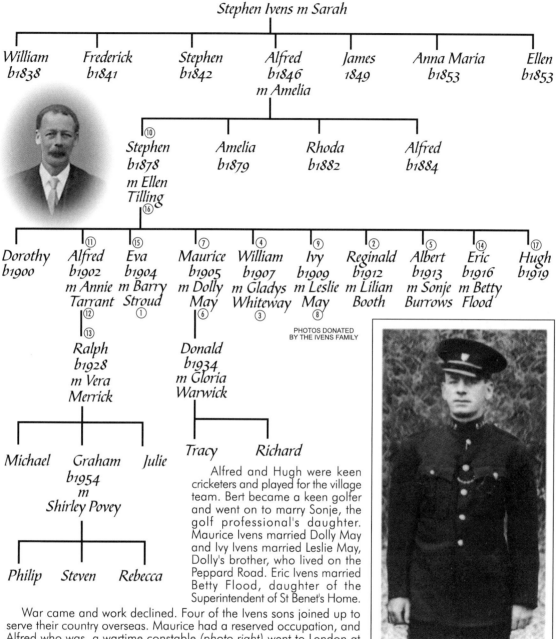

Stephen Ivens m Sarah

William b1838   Frederick b1841   Stephen b1842   Alfred b1846 m Amelia   James 1849   Anna Maria b1853   Ellen b1853

Stephen ⑩ b1878 m Ellen Tilling ⑯   Amelia b1879   Rhoda b1882   Alfred b1884

Dorothy b1900   Alfred ⑪ b1902 m Annie Tarrant ⑫   Eva ⑮ b1904 m Barry Stroud ①   Maurice ⑦ b1905 m Dolly May ⑥   William ④ b1907 m Gladys Whiteway ③   Ivy ⑨ b1909 m Leslie May ⑧   Reginald ② b1912 m Lilian Booth   Albert ⑤ b1913 m Sonje Burrows   Eric ⑭ b1916 m Betty Flood   Hugh ⑰ b1919

Ralph ⑬ b1928 m Vera Merrick

Donald b1934 m Gloria Warwick

PHOTOS DONATED
BY THE IVENS FAMILY

Michael   Graham b1954 m Shirley Povey   Julie

Tracy   Richard

Philip   Steven   Rebecca

Alfred and Hugh were keen cricketers and played for the village team. Bert became a keen golfer and went on to marry Sonje, the golf professional's daughter. Maurice Ivens married Dolly May and Ivy Ivens married Leslie May, Dolly's brother, who lived on the Peppard Road. Eric Ivens married Betty Flood, daughter of the Superintendent of St Benet's Home.

War came and work declined. Four of the Ivens sons joined up to serve their country overseas. Maurice had a reserved occupation, and Alfred who was a wartime constable *(photo right)* went to London at night to help clear bomb damage and fire fighting.

Stephen died shortly after the war and it was Alfred who re-built the firm to its pre-war eminence. In 1949 he had the opportunity to purchase a block of four cottages with extensive gardens along the Kidmore End Road. The business moved to new premises at the rear, and in time the cottages were to provide living accommodation for various members of the Ivens family. Around this time Maurice's son Donald became an apprentice in the family business and in due course father and son set up their own establishment called M & D G Ivens, building contractors. When Alfred retired in 1967, the building side of his business closed, but Bert and Hugh, the two youngest brothers, continued to work as painters and decorators under the name of A J Ivens.

Alfred's son, Ralph had a varied career away from the village, at one time running the Coach and Horses pub at Binfield Heath, and subsequently establishing the 'Homecraft' store in Caversham. He had returned in 1972 to one of the cottages his father had bought.

Hugh Ivens lived (until he died in 2002) in the house along Kidmore End Road where he was born. Graham Ivens followed the family tradition by entering the building trade, and also lives in Kidmore End Road where so much of his family history belongs.

Village People and Memories

Throughout this book it is the memories of local people that help bring it to life, and these pages pay tribute to some of them, either for their contribution to village life, or for what they recall. The Fishers and the Ivens have been detailed on preceding pages, and the Eynotts' name was prevalent throughout the 19th century, but there are other surviving names that have a long history. The oldest of these is Povey, which can be found in the 1851 census. Mrs Povey and her niece Miss Stella Povey still reside in the heart of Emmer Green. Some of the others listed in the 1929 street directory - Long, Harris, Heather, Squires, Bell, Briant, Mortimer, - are families that either have descendants still living in the area, or have recently left it.

Thomas Bew married **Elizabeth Townsend** in 1855 and set up home at Grove Cottages to start their family of nine children. They moved to the centre of the village about 1870. The first of their children was Susannah (Susan), who became well-known as the verger of Emmer Green church. Susan was encumbered for many years with a leg-brace and, as she grew older, with failing eyesight. A devout and kindly lady, she never married, but lived at Pond House, a property tucked round behind the White Horse yet quite separate from the inn until the 1940s. Some of the other family members moved away from the village when they grew up. Bertha Bew (1871-1949) was the last of the Bew family in Emmer Green and she is still remembered as a schoolteacher at the village school and in Caversham. Mr Robert Price recalls Pond House from the 1940s when he stayed there with his Great Aunt Bertha. At the bottom of the garden, which ran down to the pond was a pig-sty. Pond House still exists, a shadow of the happy family home it once was. Physically joined to the White Horse now, the downstairs serves as the inn's kitchen. William Bew (born 1873) and his brother Harry (born 1876) both fought in the Boer War and rejoined the army at the outbreak of the Great War in 1914. William died in October 1914 and is commemorated on the memorial in St Barnabas Church. Harry survived the war unscathed and subsequently married Elizabeth Fletcher whose parents were said to have run the Black Horse public house. William always enjoyed a drink in the White Horse, whereas Harry went to the Black Horse for his refreshment.

The Bew Family

PHOTO DONATED BY ROBERT PRICE

William Bailey who was born in 1872 and lived all his life in Emmer Green must have been one of the very first pupils at the old Emmer Green School in Grove Road. His parents paid 2d a week for his education, as free schooling had not then been introduced. He left school at the age of 12 years and worked at Caversham Grove house for 3/- per week. His job was to collect the eggs, vegetables, fuel and kindling. Many times his ears were boxed for not being quick enough on the job. He went on to work on the railway where he remained for fifty-four years, retiring at the age of seventy.

The **Hunt Family** (*photo below*) moved to Emmer Green 1889, when Mr Hunt took up employment as a farm bailiff for Mr Saunders of Caversham Grove. Mr Hunt was able to buy a pony and trap from a poacher, in lieu of his poaching fine. Gilbert Lawrence (Laurie) was four at the time and remembered his father carrying him up to Emmer Green from Reading Station. He subsequently attended the school in Grove Road where he was appointed to ring the bell daily. Childhood days were spent playing in King's Field beyond the pond, or skating if the pond froze. After he left school, Laurie started work at Caversham Grove as a gardener's boy, where one of his duties was maintaining a water supply from the well, with the aid of a retired carriage horse, for both Caversham Grove and the nearby houses. The water was delivered in pails hanging from wooden yokes, either by Laurie himself, or fetched by the women from the cottages. Laurie remembers there

were very few lights, no transport and sparse amenities. There was one shop only at Emmer Green, the village blacksmith belonging to David Turner, where the horses were shod, and the local builder W N & E Fisher. Apart from the fishmonger's horse and trap and an occasional delivery van, the housewife had to walk to Caversham or Reading. There was once a magnificent avenue of walnut trees in the grounds of Caversham Grove. Grove Park was opposite the house and contained the rick-yard. There were hay-ricks, pens for chickens, turkeys, guinea fowl and ducks, all of which belonged to Mr Saunders. Laurie said, that apart from the difficulties of daily life, the old countryside could not be easily forgotten.........the sight of men and women haymaking on the farms, and rakes and forks in full swing at King's Meadow.

PHOTO HIGHDOWN COLLECTION

The Hurn Family

The parents of **Alice Hurn** were butler/valet and cook to the Nobles of Hill House. They married in 1893 the wedding breakfast was held at the house. Mr Hurn was accomplished at fishing, shooting, rowing, sailing and hunting and would pass on these skills to visiting young men. Alice was the first baby to be christened at St Barnabas Church ('The Tin Tabernacle') and it was the Reverend Howe who went on to prepare her for her Confirmation and who drove with her and three other Emmer Green girls in a carriage down to St Peter's, the parent church. Unfortunately Rev Howe was profoundly deaf, leading to frequent misunderstandings, to the amusement of the children. Alice also paid tribute to Susan (Susannah Bew) who dedicated her life to duties in the church. She described the 'Green Girls' who wore long green dresses, white pinafores, white mop caps with a twin poke at the back and regularly attended church on Sundays. Alice also recalled a way of speaking, special to the area, and long since vanished. On being warned of the folly of drinking warm beer, one workman replied, "Bad Sir; there bain't no bad beer. There's just some's better than t'other."

William Bell made his money from setting up and running the Reading Football Pools in the 1920s. He lived at The Elms, Kidmore End Road (later re-developed as Twin Oaks), was married to Catherine and they had seven children. Mrs Bell had a domineering nature, but was well regarded in the village and did a lot to help organise events, plays and concerts.

One of their sons, John (Bib), married Mary, the daughter of Edwin Fisher (the village blacksmith) and his wife Ethel. Bib and Mary's daughter, Susan and her family still live in the locality. Edwin and Ethel had three daughters and it was May, Mary's younger sister, who died accidentally falling down the stairs at Fisher's yard.

The family also bought property throughout in Emmer Green and rented it out. Because they had money, and because they didn't join in the sporting activities of the lads in the village, it tended to set them apart, at a time before many professionals and businessmen had moved into the area. Bib Bell is remembered dashing about the area in an MG sports car, and telling of his war-time exploits in the RAF. Another son, Bob, had the job of making sure the street lamps in Reading were set to come on at the right time, and it was he who owned the land where Bell Court now stands.

Geoffrey Mortimer, born 1932, was the younger son of the landlord and landlady of the White Horse. As a child he befriended one of the regulars, a gentleman from Binfield Heath called Fred Wyles, who worked at the old brick kiln. Adjoining the pub garden, there used to be an old thatched cottage belonging to the Fidlers. Geoffrey's elder brother, Michael, had a passion for lighting bonfires and Mrs Fidler would come running round to complain about this to his parents, perhaps fearing a spark would set fire to her thatched roof. He also related a tragic event at The Oratory School, that occurred in the late 1930s. A couple of pupils gained possession of a rifle which they took out into the grounds. Horseplay followed resulting in an accidental firing of the gun. The injured boy died within a few days, and was buried in the grounds of Caversham Park. Reg Dearlove, a customer at the White Horse and witness to the incident, was greatly shocked. During the war one family of evacuees stayed briefly at The White Horse, whilst many others stayed in houses along Kidmore End Road and the Peppard Road. Geoffrey was the postman for Emmer Green in the 1950s.

Len Miller, born in 1936, lived with his parents and brother in Grove Road. One of his first memories was of going to the church hall with his gasmask. He recalled his father, who as a train driver had a reserved occupation, kept chickens in the war and Harry Clark, a neighbour, kept pigs on a plot of land nearby. He remembered the bombers all going over in formation and the following morning the stragglers coming back with smoke trailing. The family used to get under the stairs if the siren went. There were some Canadian troops at Tanners Lane preparing for D-day. In Grove Road the gardens went down onto a field and some Canadians came up the garden path and asked if they could have some hot water and a bit of a shave.

After the war change became inevitable. Many new people moved into the area and although this young and vibrant population established new community enterprises, the village lost its intimacy, and to some extent its identity. Only a few of the original villagers are now left, and it was fortunate that these experiences were recorded in time. Childhood memories are often the most vivid, and it is those that we have relied on here.

Celebrations

PHOTO FISHER COLLECTION

A noteable event here in 1897 was a special high tea, attended by practically the whole village, to celebrate Queen Victoria's Diamond Jubilee. Three years later an enormous oak tree was felled to commemorate the Relief of Mafeking (see p75). For the Coronation Day celebrations in honour of King Edward VII William Fisher had a huge bonfire built on the village green, at least fifty feet high. In the base he had a seat built, so that he could sit and guard the pyre until the time came for it to be lit after dark. However, inactivity being William's weak point, he soon delegated guard duties to two of his men.

In 1919 after the end of World War I a victory parade was held in conjunction with the annual Emmer Green village fête. There was a parade of the returning servicemen (see p114) followed by a fancy dress parade. Margory Akerman recalled her father organising it, and having to get up at 6am with his megaphone to wake everyone up.

At the end of World War II a huge bonfire was built on the field by the pond where the whole village assembled for a party with dancing round the bonfire. Mrs Bell organised a 'Victory' concert for the children of the village in the church hall.

The Coronation of Queen Elizabeth II was marked by a very special party in 1953 (main photo). In fact the Emmer Green Social Club and the British Legion combined to give what was believed to be the grandest and most orderly children's Coronation party in the borough. It was held on Saturday 6th June 1953 and 670 children were invited. The proceedings were opened by Mayor Cllr F H Lewis, followed by a fancy dress and decorated prams parade. Children's sports were followed by tea, where the youngsters sat at tables laid out in the shape of an 'E'. The feast included a 60lb Coronation cake, and each child was given a Coronation souvenir mug. After tea the annual fête was held followed by dancing to the music of the British Legion No10 band.

PHOTO READING MUSEUM SERVICES - BERKSHIRE CHRONICLE COLLECTION

Coronation of George VI 1937

Children's Victory Concert 1945

Tredegar Road Street Party and Parade 1977

It was 1977 that gave Emmer Green the chance to put the flags out again, when the Queen celebrated her Silver Jubilee. This time the focus was on individual street parties - Crawshay Drive, Yarnton Close, Scott Close and Tredegar Road were just a few that organised special events, games and parades. Tables were erected in the road and food laid out. Thankfully the rain kept away.

In 1995 it was The Black Horse that commemorated the fiftieth anniversary of VE day by crossing their windows with masking tape and raising the Union Jack.

The year 2000 allowed community groups to apply for grants to pay for projects to mark the new Millennium. Emmer Green took full advantage of this through out the year. Highdown School restored an Edwardian walled garden; Emmer Green Residents' Association published a leaflet and organised an exhibition, attended by many people; Friends of Clayfied Copse arranged a summer Woodlands Day with rural crafts, woodland demonstrations and guided walks; The Caversham and District Floral Society was sponsored locally, and put on a magnificent Flower Festival at St Barnabas Church. The theme was 'The History of Emmer Green'.

The year 2002 marked Queen Elizabeth II's Golden Jubilee. St Barnabas Church celebrated the day with a special luncheon in the church itself, and their annual garden party in July had a Jubilee theme.

50th Anniversary of VE Day 1995

Wilfred Owen's Family

Wilfred Owen is now regarded as the most important writer of war poetry in the English language (published in two anthologies - 'Minds at War', and 'Out in the Dark'). He was born in Oswestry in March 1893, the eldest child of Tom and Susan Owen. From early childhood he was writing verse and dreamt of becoming a poet. He was influenced by Keats and Shelley, and other nineteenth century writers. Lack of family funds denied Wilfred the university education he desired. For a short period he became assistant to the vicar at Dunsden church, but after much torment decided Christianity was inconsistent with science and poetry and left. It was during this period however that he established a close bond with his cousin, Leslie Gunston, who lived in the parish of Kidmore End. They would write poetry together.

Wilfred was studying in southern France when the First World War broke out and he made no immediate attempt to return home. By 1916, however, his conscience had got the better of him and he enlisted, and was commissioned as a second lieutenant in the Manchester Regiment. His initial experiences of action left him 'shell-shocked' and requiring medical treatment. While in hospital he met Siegfried Sassoon, and conversations they engaged in inspired him to write his war poetry. He also met the poet Rupert Graves, and after his discharge from hospital was introduced to Arnold Bennet and H G Wells. After an initial period of re-training he was deemed fit for action and returned to the trenches in September 1918. He was recommended the Military Cross for helping to clear the Hindenburg line, but was sadly killed in action on the Oise-Sambre Canal just four days before the Armistice was signed.

Apart from passing through the village to reach Dunsden, or to visit his cousin near Kidmore End, Wilfred Owen had no direct connection with Emmer Green. It was some seven years after his death, after his father had retired, that Tom and Susan Owen together with their daughter Mary settled into a house along the Peppard Road (opposite the entrance to Caversham Park House). They were to remain there for the rest of their lives, but it wasn't until Mary, Wilfred's sister, died in 1956 that an astonishing discovery was made. Susan Owen had kept every word written by her son since early childhood - a total of 554 letters. The fact they all survived was miraculous because of the careless nature in which they were kept. The family were great hoarders, keeping all manner of things, and then forgetting where they were. There was no sense of order and precious keepsakes and letters were mixed in with receipted bills and inconsequential mail. There was no chronological order, and no meticulous packaging. Bundles were found amongst needlework, in a sealed tea chest, in boxes in a garden shed. Mary had instructed that upon her death, one particular nailed-down box should be opened by the Emmer Green boy scouts. In it they found Wilfred's heavy army revolver, loaded with a pouch of live ammunition. It was this event that inspired Grevel Lindop to write his poem 'The Legacy: Emmer Green 1956'. Tom, Susan and Mary Owen are buried in Dunsden churchyard.

The Legacy: Emmer Green, 1956
by Grevel Lindop

Let the boy try. The chisel's edge is slid
into the crack. A few businesslike knocks
should do it. Gently now. The blistered lid
resists, resists. He levers at the box.

I hold it steady. (All day long they've worked
to sort Miss Mary's things. A magpie-nest
of clothes, toys, jewellery, papers, bills, that lurked
in bags, chests, cupboards, clocks; and with the rest,

I'm told, the poet's letters, stuffed in absurd
odd corners. They asked us to have a go
at these old trunks and crates. Why she left word
the Scouts should open this, I'll never know.)

A splintering crack. It gives. A musty cover
of cloth, and under it the dull green
nubbed bulk of a fully-loaded revolver.
Army issue. Nineteen-seventeen.

Thirty corroded live rounds in a pouch
of mouldy leather. Gasping, the lads crowd in.
Treasure trove! No, No: better not touch.
Steadying my hands, I pack the things again.

In mildewed lint and sour buttery tarnish
the huge unwieldy ghost of war is laid.
My fingers nearly slip on the dull varnish.
Lifting the box, I learn that I'm afraid.

From Grevel Lindop's Selected Poems,
published by Carcanet, June 2000. ISBN 1-85754-465-X

Employment

As well as the employment opportunities outlined on the following pages, many of the skilled craftsmen were employed by the Fisher family. Details of their flourishing firm and influence on the village are described on page 73.

PHOTO FISHER COLLECTION

Changing Employment Patterns

By 1871 the pattern of work in Emmer Green and the immediately surrounding area had already changed significantly from that of 20 years earlier. In common with trends across the country, agricultural employment had fallen substantially, and farm work was no longer the predominant occupation. Throughout the nineteenth century people outside the larger towns would generally have lived and worked in the same area. This included manual farm work, service in the local big houses, jobs in the brick-works and numerous trades supporting these primary occupations and the local community. Many were skilled craftsmen and the expertise was passed on down the generations - carter, blacksmith, harness-maker, carpenter, butcher, inn-keeper. Towards the end of the century, however, the proximity of Reading with its burgeoning industries, and established railway links, had already begun to alter the pattern of employment.

In the subsequent 100 years the dramatic change in the patterns of employment reflected the major trends that had been experienced everywhere by small communities located near the rapidly expanding major towns: There were three major factors involved:

★ *an overall increase in the population*
★ *a change in the character of the workforce away from the predominantly manual occupations*
★ *the increased mobility of people, allowing them to live and work in quite different places*

This latter influence was the one that had the greatest effect on the development and changing character of Emmer Green from separate village to urban suburb. By the late twentieth century the size of the population in and around the village had grown tremendously, following the large-scale house building of the 1930s and the post-war years.

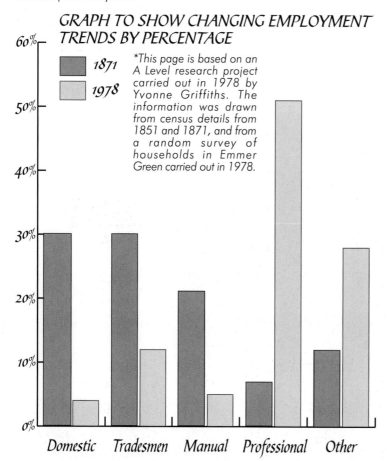

GRAPH TO SHOW CHANGING EMPLOYMENT TRENDS BY PERCENTAGE

1871
1978

*This page is based on an A Level research project carried out in 1978 by Yvonne Griffiths. The information was drawn from census details from 1851 and 1871, and from a random survey of households in Emmer Green carried out in 1978.

Domestic Tradesmen Manual Professional Other

A detailed survey in 1978 of the working population, covering one in twenty households, showed the working pattern to be very different indeed, with just over 50% employed in a professional capacity. The schools, shops and the BBC Monitoring Station provided local work opportunities, but many professionals worked in Reading, or commuted to London. Non-professional people were more inclined to work locally, and the survey also reflected the trend for married women to go out to work, even though in 1978 they opted for traditional female jobs. No doubt the intervening twenty years have continued to parallel the national trend with the increase in 'high-tech' industries in the Thames Valley, women being given equal status, and the concept of working from home in a paid capacity beginning to emerge. Another big change that can be seen from the census is that of education. In 1851 children often as young as eleven would be sent out to work on the farms or apprenticed to local tradesmen. Today sixteen is the minimum school leaving age with many youngsters continuing formal education into their early twenties.

Agriculture

Agriculture was at an employment peak in the mid-nineteenth century when everything was very labour intensive. As mechanisation was introduced, so the way of life changed taking with it the threshing gangs and thatched ricks of corn, which were such an interesting feature on the farms. The selection of crops was different then - swedes, mangel-wurzels, and large acreages of oats. Wages were very low, often as little as 20/- a week for long hours. Memories of the agricultural community in Emmer Green have been recorded and portray a very rural scene. Everyone helped at hay-making or harvesting. Wives came to help wearing white aprons and cotton bonnets. During the hot summers even the horses wore hats with their ears sticking through them. Food and refreshments were provided for the workers and a barrel of ale was kept cool under the hedge for the men to enjoy.

Workmen were invariably known by the name of their occupation. Carter was the man who travelled three times a day to the river by the old forge in Church Road, Caversham to fill an enormous barrel with water. This was perched on a cart drawn by two shire horses. They took a great pride in their work, with their well cared-for horses, and polished harnesses.

The cowman and his wife looked after the dairy herd, and their calves and pigs and chickens. In addition to plucking and dressing the chickens, the cowman's wife would cope with the offal. Wearing a voluminous white apron, she could be seen carrying a yoke from which two buckets of offal were suspended. This was then used to make sausages, faggots, lard, chitterlings and black pudding. There are also later memories of Frank Stokes, drover at Shipnell's Farm who drove the cattle from the farm down the bridle path, along the Hemdean Road, through Caversham to the cattle market, from where they were shipped abroad. It eventually ceased because of the damage the cattle caused. Milking barns (*photo page 36*) at the junction of Surley Row and St Barnabas Road, part of Grove Farm, in latter years belonged to the Co-op. Right up until the land was sold for development, Mr Roy Willis looked after the dairy herd here, where much of the area to the west was laid to pasture. On the opposite side of the road was Grove Farm house and wheat was planted in fields where Eric Avenue now stands. Milk used to be delivered to the local houses by horse and cart with big milk churns on the back, and housewives would rush out with a jug to have it filled.

In the 1930s there was a serious outbreak of foot and mouth disease, and a large pit was dug in a small field between Grove Cottages and Grove Road. The carcasses of the slaughtered animals were thrown in and covered with lime before the hole was filled in.

PHOTO HIGHDOWN COLLECTION

Smithies

Fisher's Forge

Metalwork of any kind was the blacksmith's province. The craft in Britain dates back about a thousand years and smithies were found in every village. The work included the making of horseshoes, the repair of agricultural tools, and cart metalwork. It was physically demanding work, requiring a great deal of stamina to keep the fire hot enough to heat and shape the iron, before quenching it in the trough.

The main, and oldest forge in Emmer Green stood next to The White Horse. It was generations of Eynotts who ran the smithy during the Victorian era. James was recorded as early as 1830, and by 1841 he was also publican at the inn. Ten years later he had been joined in the business by his sons Henry and James, and young Benjamin Palmer. In the late nineteenth century it was Henry and his son Harry who were the blacksmiths. It subsequently became the turn of Mr David Turner, who lived in the first cottage in School Lane. A whole team of men worked for him and it remained as a working forge until about 1932, when it was converted into a general store. One of the last working blacksmiths was Robert (Bob) Briant, a stocky man with very strong arms. He found it thirsty work necessitating frequent trips to the adjacent White Horse Inn. Bob was a popular village character, but had no hesitation in reprimanding carthorses if they turned awkward during the shoeing process.

The success of the Fisher business *(see p73)* at the end of the nineteenth century enabled them to establish their own forge with Edwin Fisher as the blacksmith. When it was founded the only means of transport was on horseback, or by horse drawn vehicles. This meant a constant demand for iron bound wheels of all kinds, horseshoes, and cart metalwork. The wheelwrights would construct the frame, then an iron band was heated to red heat in the forge, before being forced on to the outside of the wheel to contract as it cooled, so giving the wheel rigid strength and a hard wearing rim. The process was called 'burning the iron on'. The forge was still in use in the early 1930s. The blacksmith at the time, one Curly Grant, was reputed to have had his teeth knocked out by a horse he was shoeing. The building was demolished in 1988.

The Main Forge, next to The White Horse Inn

PHOTOS FISHER COLLECTION

Brick-making

At one time there would have been many small brick-kilns scattered around. Evidence on the 1844 tithe map indicates one at the top of Grove Hill, just above what is now St Agnes. The most significant kiln in Emmer Green, however, was built on land called Homer's Field in 1654 (between Kiln Road and the Peppard Road). Dr Plott, in his Natural History of Oxfordshire, 1705, writes of brick-making in this local area".. they make a sort of brick 22 inches long and above 6 inches broad". The earliest recorded owner was Mr Francis Dormer in1842, but it is possible it was owned by the Dormer family as far back as 1759. By the middle of the nineteenth century it had passed to John Leach who was responsible for building the brick kiln cottages. It then fell into the hands of Ebenezer Ward, followed in 1891 by Mr A C Brewerton. Brewerton and Stevens, as it subsequently became, lasted until 1928. By 1935 it was The Caversham Brick and Tile Works Ltd, and the last entry was made in 1947. The brickworks provided local employment, mainly in the summer, and twelve thousand bricks were made there each day. A team of nine men could produce a thousand bricks a day, for which they were each paid sixpence. The claypits lay behind the kiln works and huge pits were dug out. The coppiced woodland opposite provided a good source of fuel. The clay was loaded on to little trucks which ran on rails back to the brickyard to enter the crusher and the mixer. Long bars of clay emerged and a manually operated cutting machine cut the bars into nine bricks. A barrow load was thirty-six bricks. Tiles were also made at the yard, and there was a potter who made ornamental flowerpots and gargoyles. (For many years a dragon adorned Emmer Green Post Office). The hours were long -often a twelve hour shift, and the brick-kiln whistle sounded four times a day.

Brick Kiln Workers circa 1910

Emmer Green bricks were used beyond the immediate area, and one particular site was in the village of Nuneham Courtenay (between Dorchester and Oxford). Twice weekly the driver of the horse and cart would load up with bricks, spend the whole day transporting them to the location, unload, rest for the night and return the next day. However, this was deemed inefficient and the owner of the brick works invested in a steam wagon, fired by coal and wood. Although the driver had to stop at Woodcote for fuel, he was at least able to make the return journey.

Brickwall House was built in the early 18th century as four-roomed cottage for the brickfield foreman. It was enlarged and altered on several occasions over the years, and had a magnificent Magnolia tree against the east wall of the house, which came from the grounds of Rosehill House, and was planted in about 1889. It was occupied by Charles Stevens whilst the kiln was in operation. After the war this house was lived in by Dr Hetherington, one of the doctors at the Priory Avenue practice in Caversham. The land was finally cleared in 1980 to make way for the sheltered housing development, Wordsworth Court. Brickwall Cottages were originally the office and stables for the horses used on the brickfield.

Service

The big houses in and around Emmer Green were still a primary source of employment in the 19th century. The copy of the plan of part of the ground floor of Caversham Park mansion shows a vast amount of space set aside for those running the house. There would have been plenty to do just maintaining the properties and supporting the lifestyles of the wealthy and their visitors. Often staff directly involved lived on the premises, or in tied cottages on the estates. A typical summary would have been - butler, footman, coachman, groom, ladies maid, cook, housemaid, kitchen maid. These are all listed in the census of the day. The gardeners, usually lived away from the house itself.

The parents of Miss Alice Hurn were at one time butler/valet and cook at Hill House. She describes the daily routine of not only them, but other staff. Lighting was still by oil lamp and these would be lit by the footman. Coal fires provided all the heating, and baths were taken in bedrooms. All the water had to be carried by hand in big brass cans. Joints of meat were cooked on a jack in front of the kitchen fire, a huge fireplace with an oven either side. Meals were always formal, with dinner served under chandeliers with candles, and silver candlesticks on the table. Sidney Gibbs was for many years the gardener and a first class workman. Not only did he maintain herbaceous borders, rose beds and immaculate lawns, but in the conservatories he grew camelias, stephanotis, orchids and other sensitive plants. There was also a fern house, and in the greenhouses he grew tomatoes and cucumbers. Charles James was gardener at Caversham Grove and when he took it on in 1921, it was a wilderness, having been neglected for many years. He set about restoring the gardens and was so valued, that he was kept on after the estate passed out of private hands.

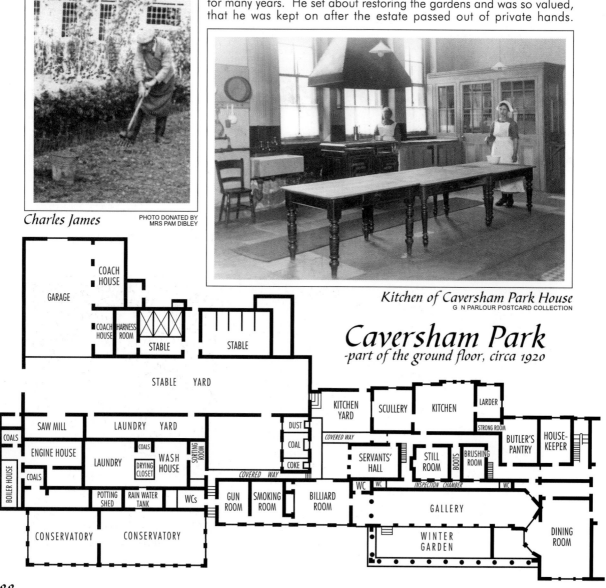

Charles James   PHOTO DONATED BY MRS PAM DIBLEY

Kitchen of Caversham Park House
G N PARLOUR POSTCARD COLLECTION

Caversham Park
-part of the ground floor, circa 1920

Laundries

Laundering clothes, before the days of the washing machine was a time consuming and skilled occupation. It was a useful way for some households to earn extra money, and ranged from those who 'took in washing' to proper businesses.

Belle Vue Hand Laundry

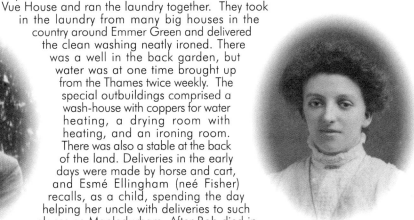

A hand laundry was run for nearly seventy-five years in Emmer Green. After beginning a laundry service from property on the corner of Kidmore End Road and Peppard Road, Belle Vue Hand Laundry (70 Kidmore End Road) was set up in 1878 by William Fisher for a relative, a Mrs Dinah Fewster, a widow with six children. Her unmarried daughter Harriet, worked in the laundry and in time took it over. Another of her daughters, Mary, married William Short, a draper in Southampton. Mary Short eventually returned to Emmer Green to help with the laundry, and it was her son Robert (Bob) and daughter, Daisy, who succeeded. Daisy and Bob, who were both unmarried, lived at Belle Vue House and ran the laundry together. They took in the laundry from many big houses in the country around Emmer Green and delivered the clean washing neatly ironed. There was a well in the back garden, but water was at one time brought up from the Thames twice weekly. The special outbuildings comprised a wash-house with coppers for water heating, a drying room with heating, and an ironing room. There was also a stable at the back of the land. Deliveries in the early days were made by horse and cart, and Esmé Ellingham (neé Fisher) recalls, as a child, spending the day helping her uncle with deliveries to such places as Mapledurham. After Bob died in 1947 Daisy kept the laundry going until about 1954. She died in 1964, aged eighty-two years.

Bob Short

Daisy Short

PORTRAIT PHOTOS FROM THE FISHER COLLECTION

The Stable Block

PHOTOS BY JONATHAN FARMER

Belle Vue House in 2000

BBC Monitoring Service

Whilst outside the official boundary of Emmer Green, its proximity to it and impact on local people is such that its history is worth recording. The BBC Monitoring Service was founded in 1939 and based at Evesham, Worcestershire. The mansion at Caversham Park and 109 acres of land were bought from The Oratory School in 1942 for £55,000, and by April 1943 staff had moved in and operational services were moved without interruption.

BRITISH
BROADCASTING
CORPORATION

CAVERSHAM
PARK

An extensive aerial system at Crowsley Park collected the signals, which were then transferred by a landline to Caversham Park. For the rest of the War 'news' and 'intelligence' was provided for all government departments with a direct link to Winston Churchill and the War Cabinet. A partnership was forged with its US counterpart, the Foreign Broadcast Information Service, which still continues. By the end of the war staff numbers had risen to 1000, many of those being foreign nationals with language skills. Very few local people had knowledge of, or were aware of the true significance of these operations. Those households that had staff billeted upon them, might have known more than most, but there was national security to consider and the details were not divuldged. Peace-time surveillance funded by the Foreign Office still kept on half the workforce, and the Monitoring Station played a significant rôle during the Cold War and events such as the Cuban Missile Crisis, the Gulf War and crises in the former Yugoslavia.

Private Telephone Exchange 1945 -supervised by Minty Moony
PHOTO COURTESY OF THE BBC

Main Listening Room 1950 -used up until 1989, when new West Wing opened
PHOTO COURTESY OF THE BBC

To this day they still maintain the policy of reporting foreign news media, comprehensively and accurately without bias or comment. Today not only does radio have to be monitored, but terrestrial and satellite television, the press, news agency reports and the Internet. This covers 150 different countries and 100 different languages. Computerisation has helped achieve this and a new West Wing listening room was opened in 1989. The BBC's official written archives are located in a building along the Peppard Road. The recently formed Radio Berkshire transmits from Caversham Park.

Sport & Recreation

The Park

Hospital Sunday 1918

As late as the early 1860s large commons existed in the Caversham area, including the one at Emmer Green. The 1865 'inclosure award' attempted to take these away from the people in a ruthless way. The little cricket ground at Emmer Green was awarded to a landowner, subject to the right of the people to use it for recreation, but the freehold was sold and the puchaser attempted to close the ground to the public. Certain heroic spirits, however, asserted their rights, and, despite proceedings before the Henley Bench of Magistrates, they gained the day, and the Emmer Green recreation ground remained the only place for outside amusement in the parish. Every year several fairs were held on this great open space, and a massive bonfire was built to celebrate the Coronation of Edward VII (see p80). The original fencing around the land was pulled down in 1911, and for over 20 years it stood as unfenced common land. Although it was rough ground, cricket and football used to be played, and a quoits area was set up on the corner of Grove Road and Kidmore End Road. Gypsies frequently camped there and caused annoyance to local residents. At this time much of the ground on the Grove Road side was marshy land, and reeds and rushes grew in the ditches that crossed it. Reading Corporation assumed the responsibility after the war, tidied up the land, installed an effective drainage system, and fenced off the park area. Steam fairs and fêtes were held there during the 1950s, and the park always seemed to be

full of children playing. In June 1953 a big party was held to celebrate the Coronation of Queen Elizabeth II (see p80).

Autumn 1993

Winter 1985

Today the park is quieter, but still home to impromptu games and pastimes, particularly in the summer, and the long tradition of football continues through autumn and winter. A children's play area occupies the northern corner, the original equipment being replaced 1993, the design being chosen by local schoolchildren.

Spring 2000

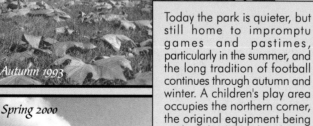

Summer 1985

Rugby

The Old Redingensians Rugby Football Club (former Reading School pupils) was born in 1924. For the first few years the club rented various sites in Reading, but during the 1926/7 season a decision was made to purchase their own ground. A convenient plot of 19½ acres off Grove Road, Emmer Green had aroused some interest, and £800 was needed to acquire it. A combination of fund-raising and loans from the RFU enabled the transaction to go ahead. There was space on the

ORRFC XV, 1927

PHOTO OLD REDINGENSIAN ARCHIVES

land for two rugby pitches, a cricket square, and grazing by livestock. Eventually baths were installed at The White Horse and the club maintained its headquarters there. There were six baths on the ground floor and the changing room was above. At the time Ernest Mortimer was landlord, and it was his duty to ensure that the coke boiler was well stoked up on Saturday match days.

By the time the team was ready to start playing at their new ground in 1927, they had already notched up several successful seasons and were establishing a good reputation. At the official opening of the new ground on 1st October 1927, F H Stokes, international rugby player from the 1870s and former president of the RFU, was invited to 'kick off'. Old Redingensians went on to beat their opponents Thames Valley. E K Pope was captain during this season and the playing membership increased to sixty, with a second team turning out about a dozen times. By now financially secure, a full fixture list was arranged for three sides for the 1928-9 season. D G Francis, one of the very early players, was able to bring a series of visiting XVs to play at Emmer Green. In 1929-30 he brought a team of Internationals, Blues and London Welsh led by W Roberts, the Oxford University captain and Welsh fly half. Two more teams came in the thirties to play teams made up of Old Redingensians and Berkshire Wanderers and another played the Berkshire county team. By 1937 the Old Redingensians were a big noise in Berkshire, seven of them representing the county against Middlesex. In 1939 Mr G H Keaton, Headmaster of Reading School and President of the Rugby Club since its inauguration, retired, marking the end of an era. Mr C E Kemp took over, but activities had to be suspended due to the war.

In 1945, Old Redingensians Rugby Football Club re-emerged with a string of successsful games and a number of players appeared for their county, but their days at Emmer Green were numbered. The Borough Council, desperate for housing after the war, had earmarked the Grove Road ground for development. Their persistence paid off, and in 1948 they paid just over £5000 to purchase the land. Eventually in 1950 a new site was found off the London Road in Sonning, where the club were able to set up enhanced facilities and build a proper clubhouse.

PHOTO READING MUSEUM SERVICES
- BERKSHIRE CHRONICLE COLLECTION

Football

Football must have been played in Emmer Green for over one hundred years, for the photograph on the right shows the team in 1894. Members of the Fisher family were always active participants in the sport and Roy Fisher and his sister Esmé recall great excitement when their father, George, played in two cup finals on the same day! The photograph below, right of the **Emmer Green Young Men's Society Fooball Club** 1903-04, includes the young George Fisher as Vice-Captain of the team *(back, 3rd from left)*. George King was the Captain *(front row, middle)*.

Very little is recorded of the team in its early days, but it was reformed in 1949, when things started to get back to normal after the war. George Fisher again played a prominent rôle, this time as Chairman. His son Roy was elected Secretary. Every Annual General Meeting, usually held in The White Horse, was minuted and recorded, right up until 1989, and these give an insight into the running of the club, and for some years, the fortunes of the team.

It was initially called the **Emmer Green Villa Football Club**, but shortly became the **Emmer Green Football Club**. Team colours were green and

PHOTO BERKSHIRE RECORD OFFICE - MARY KIFT COLLECTION

PHOTO FISHER COLLECTION

white, and when the club was formed there were no vacancies in the Reading and District League, so they had to join the Ascot and District League, until a place became available. This meant hiring a Smith's coach for players and supporters to travel to away matches. The team, who were often entertained to tea and cake after the matches, reciprocated after home games, as Mrs Bell would lay on refreshments in the Iron Room. After the war the recreation ground had become a somewhat swampy area and football was not possible,

Emmer Green Football Team 1955

PHOTO DONATED BY GEORGE HARRIS

but the team was allowed to play on one of the fields of Park Farm. George Fisher offered to lend some goal posts, whilst the army were contacted to supply old camouflage netting to use as goal nets. On a Saturday match day Roy Fisher would finish work in the Fisher yard at 12 noon, then go over to the football pitch, set up the goals and mark up the lines with a chalk line marker. After lunch he returned to play in the match. Other members were Tommy & Peter White, Bobby Barnes, Hugh Ivens, and Perry Diggins. Roy was joined in the team by brother Bill, and Bill's son Barry. Phyllis Fisher was the team's official first-aider.

The team used to change in the old Iron Room along Kidmore End Road until Mr Mortimer, landlord of The White Horse allowed them to strip down and wash in the former stables. Later the changing facilities moved to the old school house in Grove Road. In due course the pitch moved to the recreation ground, but this was not without its problems, and it wasn't until 1984 that the drainage was finally sorted with the Council spending £15,000 laying underground pipes. This meant the facility was lost for a season, but soon afterwards the club achieved their longstanding ambition when the Council funded (£40,000) the building of new changing facilities behind one of the goal areas.

The team was funded by subscription and various local social fundraising events and outings. There was often difficulty persuading team members to cough up money - in 1983, 45 team members signed up, with only 12 actually paying. Financial matters were made worse if the club were fined for offences on the field, such as in 1979, when this amounted to £43! The following year, however, the team played in fancy dress in a charity game against The Black Horse Bristols and raised £74 for the Ken Thomas Scanner Appeal.

The highest achievement of the team was to reach the final of the Berks and Bucks Junior Cup, but were sadly beaten by Theale 3-1. Frank Clayson, landlord of The White Horse was President from 1954-1971, and in 1959, the Frank Clayson Charity Shield Cup was set up, with matches against Kidmore End played annually on Boxing Day. In 1962/3 the funds raised were in aid of kidney research in recognition of the kidney donation of Dr Charles Spencer (see p60). Otherwise the proceeds were given to St Benet's Home.

1966 was reported as a good year with team spirits high as they came 4th in Division 3 of the Reading League, earning promotion to Division 2, and reaching the third round of both the Town and the Junior Cup The next season saw them struggle in the higher division, but they ended up 6th, comfortably avoiding relegation. Players of the seventies included Barry Fisher, Kevin Eighteen, John Garner, and Roger Wells. During this period Emmer Green signed the footballing superstar "Roy of the Rovers" (photo right), or rather his creator, local author Tom Tully. It was joked that "Roy" had had to lower his sights from the dizzy heights of Melchester Rovers, but provided Tom got his pint in The Black Horse after the match, the lack of transfer fees didn't bother him! The photo on the right shows the team in the 1972 Division 2 play-offs against Davis Street. The result was a draw, with Wells scoring Emmer Green's only goal. By 1985 the first team was promoted to Division 1, and the next year under Trevor Dymond's leadership they got to the quarter final of the Reading Junior Cup, with the reserves reaching the final of the Subsidiary Cup.

After being Secretary for nearly twenty years Roy Fisher handed over to his nephew Barry, but it was Christine Fisher who undertook the task for a further seven years. By the mid-late 1970s the Fisher family were taking a lesser part in the running of the club, although Bill

PHOTOS FROM THE FISHER COLLECTION

Fisher remained as Chairman until his death in 1985, and his wife Gwendoline, known as Babs, went on to complete 40 years of laundering the kit in 1989. Trevor Dymond eventually took over as Secretary and kept the club going until 1990.

In 2000 the Emmer Green football team was playing in the 3rd Division of the Sunday League. It was sponsored by The Black Horse, managed by Steve Cowan, and the Secretary was Catherine White.

Cricket

Archives have revealed that the **Emmer Green Cricket Club** started playing as far back as 1880, with a win against Stoke Row on July 10th. Regular matches were played on the recreation ground, some against teams with very unusual names such as 'Dawn of the Day CC', 'Peep of the Day CC' and 'Why Not CC'! By 1899 Emmer Green was able to join the Reading and District League, reaching the final of the Cohen Cup, but losing to Grovelands CC. Apart from the war years, the club continued to play in either the first or second division right up until 1934. Memories remain of the team being transported by horse and cart to play opposing teams in the local area. By the end of that decade existing team members were becoming too old to continue, and any potential new recruits were off to war. The team disbanded.

PHOTO FISHER COLLECTION

PHOTO DONATED BY JOHN DARBY

Cricket Team circa 1910

It wasn't until 1947 that the team were ready to re-form, but by then the park had been fenced off, and the game of cricket banned. Limited facilities were available on land on the other side of the Peppard Road, but for serious cricket the team had to go down to King's Meadow in Caversham. The British Legion provided funds for equipment etc. and the team became known as the **Emmer Green British Legion Cricket Team.** In the beginning they would play against other local teams - Stoke Row, Peppard, Ipsden, and in time, as more members got their own cars, they ventured further to contest teams from places like Aldershot.

By 1958 the recreation ground at Clayfield Copse became established and the team moved there. In the early 1960s Haddock's the builders were developing Rosehill Park and offered a redundant pavilion belonging to The Oratory Preparatory School to the Emmer Green Cricket Team, if they undertook to move it to the site themselves. It had to be dismantled and reassembled within a couple of days. All members of the team worked valiantly to achieve this, offering a variety of skills in the process. Les Sutton was the foreman. Later mains electricity was introduced. The pavilion remained and served the club well, until its demise by vandals in 1979 (photo p97).

President's XI 1963

PHOTO DONATED BY JOHN DARBY

1981 Division 5 Champions

PHOTOS RAY SPACKMAN

Fire damaged Cricket Pavilion

The Council provided a temporary pavilion, and as a result of joint effort by a number of bodies the 'Ken Barrington' pavilion was built and opened in 1981 and continues to provide excellent sporting facilities.

The building of Caversham Park brought renewed interest and by 1974 the club was able to field a second eleven. More adventurous matches were arranged including the first of many tours of the Wye Valley. The club eventually joined the Berkshire Cricket League in 1981, and played in various divisions thereafter. In its heyday the club was fielding a Wednesday side, two Saturday sides and one on Sunday. It finally closed in 1992, because whilst there were still many cricketers who wanted to play it became impossible to fill the administrative posts.

Another cricket club flourished in Emmer Green during the 1950s and 60s. It was known as the **Reading Schoolmasters' Cricket Club**. When Caversham Grove became The Grove Secondary School in 1952, provision was made for a cricket square in a field bordering Surley Row. Groundsman, 'Smudger Smith' maintained it, and several of the masters took an interest in coaching the boys. It seemed a pity the ground remained unused at weekends, and in 1955 a group of cricket playing teachers asked permission to play the occasional informal game on the field. On condition they paid the groundsman, which was agreed, a team was gathered together, and several good matches played. The club was then officially formed, with a Secretary, Alan Lander, who quickly arranged a full fixture list against the local clubs. There was a small band of local supporters and the wives provided the teas. Bill Goodworth joined and became Captain in 1956, and his team included gritty Yorkshireman Dave Berry, fast bowler Mike Keast from Stoneham School, Den Riley of Alfred Sutton School, Alan Lander, Jim Harrison of Wargrave Piggott School, and Bernard Rose of The Grove School, was wicket keeper and Treasurer. The team retired to the Gardeners' Arms after a match.

Many fine matches were played with centuries being scored by Bill Goodworth and others. The success of the club continued, and as funds built up they were able to provide themselves with all the necessary equipment, as well as two sight screens for the ground. By the 1960s it had become possible to arrange a Cricket Week on the Grove Ground after the end of each summer term. The club prospered until 1966 when many of the founder members felt it was time to retire. Unfortunately there were not enough keen young cricketing schoolmasters to keep things going, and even with a reduced fixture list they struggled, finally disbanding in 1968. Unfortunately this growing lack of enthusiasm in the schools was to have a serious impact on our once dominant national sport for many future generations.

Golf

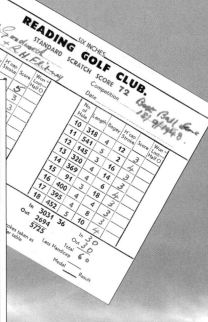

Reading Golf Club at Emmer Green was formed in August 1910, and began life as the **Caversham & South Oxon Golf Club**. Some of the founder members were wealthy local people who ensured their names would be held in perpetuity by presenting trophies to be awarded to the winners of annual competitions. The Crawshay Cup, the West Challenge Cup and the Maitland Cup were of that ilk. W T Crawshay, grandson of the Welsh Ironmaster, was the first President of the club. The Palmer Cup (Huntley & Palmers) and the Sutton Cup (Sutton Seeds) originated from the Tilehurst Golf Club, but were passed to Caversham and South Oxon when Tilehurst closed after the First World War. They are still used in Easter competitions against Sonning and Calcot Golf Clubs.

PHOTO COURTESY OF BILL GOODWORTH

There have been many changes to the course over the years. The first came with the outbreak of World War I. Apart from the financial difficulties the sudden drop in membership created for a comparatively new club, just over thirty acres of land were ploughed up under the direction of the War Agricultural Committee, and the course was reduced to nine holes. After the war the full eighteen holes were restored, but the layout was somewhat different to that of today. At one time there were three holes on 'Little Field', leased land to the east of Kidmore End Road, opposite the turning to Tanners Lane. During World War II the 7th hole was commandeered as a wheat field to help the war effort, and posts were erected to deter gliders from landing. Land has been purchased at intervals to extend and improve the course.

A man named Bishop was the first professional at the club, and for a while, he even had to fill the rôle of head greenkeeper when the original man resigned his post. The equipment for maintaining the course was very primitive by today's standards. A horse (wearing felt overshoes to protect the greens) pulled a water cart for soaking the greens in dry weather. A water pump was installed on the 14th fairway, and its foundations remained until the mid 1980s. One source of income was the sale of grass for cattle fodder, and a local farmer by the name of Chown was employed to cut it during the summer. Another was to allow sheep to graze on the course. This was something of a mixed blessing as they had a habit of falling asleep in the bunkers! Records show that at least one sheep was killed by a misdirected golf ball. From the 1930s onwards Bill Kingston was the head greenkeeper, and with his hard working assistants Joe and Archie kept the course in excellent condition.

PHOTO CLIVE ORMONDE

The first clubhouse was constructed of brick and timber, with a felt roof. There was a verandah along the front overlooking the 18th hole. The clubhouse survived the World War II bomb damage, but a spectacular blaze in 1963 destroyed it completely. Stan Peddle and Geoff King managed to rescue a few sets of clubs from the locker room, but otherwise all was lost. A temporary replacement was erected within two months, and St Benet's Home came to the rescue with the use of their sports pavilion. The 'pre-fab' lasted until 1980 when a substantial brick building was designed and built.

A complete reorganisation of the club's structure was undertaken in 1968, and a couple of years later the company was called Reading Golf Club Limited. To avoid outside influence the regulations were changed, so that only current playing members could hold shares in the club.

The Secretary of the club in the 1930s was Major H D Hawkins and he was succeeded after the war by Mr Ramsden. Successive professionals during that period were Dick Flitney, George Burrows and Pat Roberts. Pat was a bit of a mimic, and in the pre-video days could imitate with accuracy most members' swings. Cecil Haddock set up most of the existing competitions, and Bob Hodges, past Captain and stalwart committee member, conceived the idea of the Christmas Fowl & Rabbit Competition.

Exhibition Match, 1954

PHOTOS COURTESY OF READING GOLF CLUB

Club Presentation, 1965

The finest golfer produced by the club was Michael King. Starting as a junior, he went on to captain the British Youth Team, and eventually competed with the Walker Cup teams of 1969 and 1972. After turning professional he qualified to play in the Ryder Cup team of 1979. High standards of play continue and in the year 2000 several of the younger members are completing golf scolarships in the USA.

Athletics

For decades Emmer Green had been a favoured spot for cross-country runners. It wasn't until the early 1960s when local builder Mr Jack Bridges, President of Reading Athletics Club, built new premises off the Kiln Road, that a dream of forty years finally came true. He owned some land on the site of the old brickworks which was deemed unsuitable for housing. He generously donated parcels of land to several local social and sporting organisations, with the provision that it continue to be used for its original purpose. There was provision for a Rifle Club, a Boxing Club, space for the Emmer Green Social Club and for the local scout troop (see page 104). The jewel in the crown, however, was the building of the headquarters of Reading Athletics Club, which was duly opened by the Marquess of Exeter, Lord Burghley, who was President of the

Amateur Athletics Association. The official ceremony took place on 17th October 1962 and in his opening speech Lord Burghley praised Mr Bridges and urged club members to make full use of their splendid facilities. Club Chairman Mr A E Lovegrove pronounced it the greatest day in the club's history. Among the guests were international athletics competitors Mary Rand and Bruce Tulloh. The winter of 1962/3 was particularly severe, but that didn't prevent the Inter-County Cross-Country Championships, sponsored by the Daily Telegraph (photo below), taking place in the January. In the mid-1960s the National Cross-Country Championships were held at Caversham Park, based on the changing facilities at the new clubhouse.

Unfortunately, as Palmer Park became the focus for athletics in Reading, and open countryside vanished under a wave of new housing, so the interest in the Emmer Green headquarters declined, and the building fell into a state of disrepair. It finally disappeared when Wordsworth Court was built in the early 1980s.

PHOTOS READING MUSEUM SERVICES
-BERKSHIRE CHRONICLE COLLECTION

Entertainment / Social Life

The Reading Mercury of 1846 records a 'prize fight between two women in Emmer Green' for which a large crowd gathered. Years ago the villagers had to make their own entertainment. Singing and music making was important, and Emmer Green had its own band, and a team of handbell ringers. It also had its share of acting talent and put on several Minstrel Shows to entertain the community. A programme remains of a 'Miscellaneous Concert' held in The Schoolroom, Emmer Green, April 1901. Miss I Short and Mr S Gibbs played pianoforte and banjo, followed by a dozen songs and recitations. A curious play followed entitled "The Matrimonial Agency"- two of the characters include Mr Ponsonby Funkleton, and Mr Augustus Plantagenet Splatchett! When the new St Barnabas Church was completed the original was able to be used as a hall for all kinds of social events (see p70). There are newspaper reports of plays and concerts staged there throughout the 1930s. During the war years children organised their own concerts (photo above), supported by Mrs Bell.

PHOTO DONATED BY THE HARRIS FAMILY

Social Clubs

Following the post-war housing development, the **Emmer Green Social Club** was formed in 1949 to cater for the needs of the growing community. Committee meetings were held at members' homes, and the social side, under Mr Ted Smith, held events at St Barnabas Church Hall. There was dancing and cabaret, and the functions were well supported. In 1953 the club helped organise the Queen's Coronation celebrations in the park (see p80). Shortly afterwards the social club ran a fête on the recreation ground which was opened by Basil Darden, director of the film 'The Blue Lamp' and his wife, actress Melissa Darden, niece of Emmer Green resident Mrs Irene Allon. Regular fêtes took place thereafter, usually opened by the Mayor of Reading. They were attended by an average of 4000 people, with all proceeds going to St Benet's Home. One memorable event was a game of giant 'pushball'. The ball, 6ft in diameter, had to be hired from London and the two pub sides played each other. Despite erecting a safety fence the ball wandered into the crowd, landing on and injuring an unfortunate OAP. Local Authority grants were also given to enable classes in woodwork, dressmaking, painting etc to be set up. At its height, when the club was catering for about 700 families, and when Jack Bridges (photo p100) donated land off the Kiln Road to local organisations, the Emmer Green Social Club was included. However support dwindled and their allocation was eventually sold off to the scouts.

The **Rendezvous Club**, a lively evening social club for the over 50s at the North Reading Youth and Community Centre, first met in 1981. Activities include bingo, dancing, entertainment, day trips and weekends away. The **Friendship Club** is for a similar age group, but has afternoon meetings instead.

Youth Clubs

It was in the 1940s that Emmer Green had its first official youth club, started by two friends Pamela James and Edna Christopher. It had a proper committee and opened in a building in the Peppard Road, then moved to the old Iron Room on Kidmore End Road before settling for a venue in The White Horse. Fund-raising activities like dances were held and helped many local needy people. When the club finally closed surplus funds were given to the British Legion. Some twenty years later John Whitehead recalls how his rock 'n' roll band nearly blew the roof off St Barnabas Church Hall. The club was run on behalf of Reading Borough Council by Mr and Mrs Holder. It was a very popular club, but the Holders were strict on enforcing the no alcohol policy. By 1969 the need for purpose built youth facilities was recognised, and Emmer Green was chosen as the site for the North Reading area (see p70). By the early 1980s there were youth club meetings on three nights a week, and the Reading Evening Post described the place as "bubbling over with life". A typical evening's activities included snooker, football, judo, martial arts, dance practice and there was a lively coffee bar. A mixed dance troupe called Body Heat was a product of the club and one of the best of its kind in the south of England. In the year 2000 under the guidance of youth worker Steve Green and a team of dedicated volunteers, the youngsters still meet thrice weekly, with one of those evenings devoted to the Duke of Edinburgh Award scheme. Other challenges include international exchange work and community based projects.

Gardening

The **Emmer Green Gardening Club** was a branch of the Social Club which set up in 1949, after the new housing estate was built, and many of the residents were establishing and maintaining new gardens. It began life in a small hut positioned on the corner of Evesham Road and Knights Way (see *photo p67*). It was founded by Bert Rolfe, keen gardener and engine driver by profession. Such was the demand that the club soon outgrew the first shed and a new bigger building was erected

PHOTOS CLIVE ORMONDE

between Grove Road and Knights Way. The 'Garden Shed' was run and manned by volunteers and opened on Sunday mornings to sell horticultural wares to members. In winter months seeds could be ordered for the next season. Even in latter years membership was as little as 50p. The club flourished for over fifty years, until by the year 2000 demand had declined and the people running it were well past retirement age.

Allotments are defined as small plots of land not exceeding a quarter of an acre in extent, chiefly used for the cultivation of vegetables. In order to give the rural population a direct interest in the land, various Acts of Parliament were passed throughout the 19th century. The most effective one was the Allotment Act of 1887 that enabled country dwellers to rent plots of land for a very modest fee. The Grove Road allotments certainly pre-dated this, as Oxfordshire records showed that as a result of the Inclosure Exchange Act, in 1865 the Churchwardens and Overseers of the Poor were awarded rent of £1 4s 6d for the parcel of land measuring 1 acre, 2 roods and 21 perches. This land was divided into eighteen plots, which can clearly be seen on the 1877 O S map *(page 24)*. In 1921 it was considered that the rent of 4d a pole was insufficient and it was duly raised to 6d.

It was around the time that the Smallholdings and Allotment Act of 1908 was passed, that Reading Borough Council actively sought to purchase land for that purpose, even looking outside the borough. Early maps clearly show quite a large area set aside for allotments between Gravel Hill and Highdown Hill Road. They would have initially have been on part of the Rosehill Estate, but an agreement to exchange land was made with the Council. They

began to disappear in the mid-1930s when the land was required for housing. Gardening was much more of a necessity than a hobby years ago, particularly during and after the wars, when fruit and vegetables were so scarce. Later allotments were established in the areas of Greenleas Avenue, Gorselands and Pinetree Court. Only the original Grove Road allotments remained in the year 2000.

Emmer Green never had its own horticultural show, but at one time enthusiastic gardeners used to exhibit their produce at the Caversham Flower Show.

Scouts

There was an established scout group in Emmer Green before the war, which used to meet in the old Iron Room along Kidmore End Road. Boy Scout Foster Jones remembered visiting every house in the village in 1947 to collect jam-jars which were taken to the Co-op Jam factory, who paid 2d per jar. He recalled collecting thousands by bike from an area between Kidmore End Road, Peppard Road and Gravel Hill. The **89th Reading Scout** troop was founded in the early 1950s by Skipper Knight, and originally based near the Milestone Wood on Caversham Park. Another troop, the **3rd Caversham Scouts** is based at the top of Grove Hill and affiliated to St Peter's Church in Caversham.

89th Milestone Wood Scout Group

Freddie Knight 1905 - 1983. When he was eight Fred joined the cub pack attached to St John's in Caversham. From that moment scouting became his raison d'être, and he rose to become Assistant District Commissioner for North Reading. The post-war development of Emmer Green caused a huge increase in

population. The need for a scout group was recognised and in 1951 Freddie Knight was asked to form one in Emmer Green. He became Group Scout Leader and on his compulsory 'retirement' in 1965 he became the group's first President. His career was marked by awards from the Chief Scout; the Silver Acorn in 1966, and in 1982 the coveted Silver Wolf, the top scouting award. He was well known nationally and internationally throughout the scouting world, and was renowned as a campfire leader par excellence. The image of Freddie standing in the glow of the flames, wearing his camp blanket covered in badges, is an abiding memory shared by all the scouts.

Another of his specialities was the art of rope-spinning, a skill passed on to his scouts. The photograph shows one team armed with 'crinolines'. It is signed by Lord Rowallan, the Chief Scout. Freddie was confined to a wheelchair for the last few years of his life, but he still visited the '89th' and travelled abroad. It was on a visit to New Zealand in 1983 that he died, and after a memorial service there, his ashes were flown back to Emmer Green. After a ceremony at the hut they were scattered in the grounds, and a tree planted in his memory. A carved plague was unveiled, inscribed 'The Skipper Knight Scout Hut'.

ALL SCOUT PHOTOS COURTESY OF THE COUNTY SCOUT ARCHIVES

In 1951 Reading and District Scouting Association were already leasing a portion of Caversham Park as a scout camping area, and it was natural that the 89th Scouts should use the site for summer activities, adopting 'Milestone Wood' as their group name. St Barnabas Hall remained their winter base. On the site in Milestone Wood was a corrugated tin hut which became known as 'The Tabernacle'. Beside it stood the milestone London XXXVIII from which the wood got its name. Its origins date from 1764 when Lord Cadogan employed Capability Brown to redesign his park, re-routing the main drive up the valley from the Henley Road. The milestone has always been closely cherished and when Davis Estates were clearing Caversham Park for development in the 1960s they gave permission for a rescue mission. The stone now stands outside the present headquarters.

Freddie was anxious to get a more permanent base for the 89th and coincidentally, in 1959, Mr Bridges had a site available (see p100). A parent associated with the Ministry of Works procured an old Nissan hut, and parents rallied together, persuading Claude Fenton to lend them a digger, and built the foundations. Contact was made with the Territorial Army, and a team of men erected the hut 'as an exercise!'. The scouts had a site, and a potential headquarters. It took a further two years to make the hut useable and it was officially opened in May 1962.

89th Milestone Scouts 1964

Around 1970 it became apparent that the Nissan hut was inadequate and that a new hall was needed. Under the guidance of parent Nick Nicholson, a Banbury building was erected on the site officially opened in 1976 (photo left). The Emmer Green Social Club was not using a neighbouring plot and the Scouts at first leased, and later bought the plot, giving them space for outside activities and camping in the grounds. In 1976 the storage hut burned down and a second Banbury building was erected offering toilets and extra rooms, and a link to the main hall - a project completed in about 1980.

In the 1960s the group ran two cub packs, a scout group, and a senior scout group and it was a golden period. Scouts did well in the County competitions, and in 1966 no fewer than six scouts achieved the Queen's Scout Award. Fundraising efforts have included, jumble sales, annual fêtes, Christmas post delivery, and regular book sales. By the 1980s the Group was catering for over 200 boys. A beaver unit for under seven year olds was started in about 1983 by Margaret Ellison. Girls joined for the first time in 1991.

Scout Leader Colin Gamble with County Commissioner Bill Vincent 25th May 1976

In 1957 a contingent from Reading, including boys from the '89th' attended, with Skipper Knight, an International Jamboree in Sutton Coldfield. When they arrived their equipment, which had been sent on ahead by rail, had gone astray, and the party were forced to improvise, scrounging cooking equipment etc. They were given an old hut to sleep in which they immediately christened 'Hotel-de-Posh'!

Annual scout summer camps were held in all parts of the UK, including North Wales,

Guernsey and Falmouth, and in the 1970s, under the guidance of Malcolm Frew, the boys canoed in places like the Wye Valley. There have been representatives from the 89th at every World Scout Jamboree since they began. In 1997 this was in Chile, and Thailand is on the agenda for 2003.

Although not affiliated to a particular church, the scouts are represented in two parades in Reading every year. On the nearest Sunday to St George's Day they march with other groups through the town centre to a service at St Mary's Church. The autumn Armistice Day parade culminates at the war memorial in Caversham.

For many years there was a very well suported cub football team who would train under the guidance of a successsion of dedicated fathers and helpers. As well as competing against local teams, at the end of each season, the packs played each other for the Bill Clack Trophy.

A new Venture Scout unit, 'The Trogs' started in 1981 under Chris Corti. This included boys and girls, and the name was selected on the basis of the underlying caves/mines (see p8 or p10), which at one time served as the County Caving Base. The unit is one of the most successful in the district, and in 1997 they set up a new county record of seven Queen's Scout Awards.

Thanks to a dedicated team of leaders and helpers, and a supportive parents' committee, the '89th' remains one of the largest groups in the district and county. It supports 2 beaver units, 3 cub packs, 2 scout troops and 1 venture unit. The cub packs have always been particularly popular. It is a tribute to those who have followed on from Freddie Knight, that over many years they have been able to sustain the success that he initiated in the 1950s.

County Swimming Shield 1981

Guides & Brownies

PHOTO CHRISTINE HARDIE

Christine Fisher
of the
1st Emmer Green Company
As A QUEEN'S GUIDE you have
prepared yourself for service to God
and your fellowmen and have shown
yourself a true member of the great
Guide Sisterhood. This will help to
make your journey through life a
joyous adventure. I congratulate
you and wish you Godspeed.

Elizabeth R

Guides and Brownies setting off for Camp in the 1950s

The Emmer Green groups are part of the Caversham East District, which is itself part of Reading Abbey Division of the Berkshire County Guide Association. Guiding in Emmer Green has always been closely associated with St Barnabas Church. The groups have always met in the Church Hall and periodically attend parade services at the church. The Guides' sweet stall is a long-standing feature of the St Barnabas Christmas Fayre.

The **Queen's Guide Award** was set up nationally in 1946 and given to high achieving guides up until 1984. The Emmer Green Guides have a proud record of their youngsters achieving the coveted award. There have been a total of seven girls receiving the honour, the first being Christine Fisher in 1968. More recently the **Baden-Powell Awards** have gone to a further four guides.

PHOTO FRED WALKER

Christine Fisher (above) and Gwynneth Notton (right) with their Awards

The movement came to Emmer Green in 1950, and although there has been at least one guide company continuously since that time, the original **1st Emmer Green Guides** was disbanded in 1988. By then the **2nd Emmer Green Guides** had been operating for fourteen years and was able to continue and adopt the prime rôle. It was Mrs Helen Holloway who formed that group in 1974 and led it, until she left to take on the rôle of District Commissioner. Anne Sear who took over was followed by Anne-Marie Semple, Joyce Carney, Fiona McDonald, Caroline Wright and Carol Snook.

PHOTO JOHN NOTTON

1984

The **1st Emmer Green (St Barnabas) Brownie Pack** was started by Mrs Barbara Morley (assisted by Mrs Joyce Trott) in 1950, who led as Brown Owl until 1970. Three leaders followed over the next fourteen years, when Debbie Tarrant assumed the leadership, which she still holds. Some 400 girls have had a lot of fun with the pack since its inauguration. At the beginning demand was so great that a second pack, the **2nd Emmer Green Brownie Pack**, was set up in 1952 by Mrs Trott. Lorna Browning was in charge in the 1970s until her retirement in 1981. Elaine Bloomfield led for the next 11 years, until current leader Lorraine Bilsby took command.

The weekly meetings offer a wide range of activities, including games, handicrafts, First Aid, sports, hospitality skills, singing, and of course work for badges. There are also visits locally, and farther afield the summer camps, with their outdoor pursuits, are a major event in the year. The Brownies have accommodation indoors, and a favourite local location was Coddesdon Lodge *(photo above)* in the grounds of Basildon Park House. More recently the Guiding Centre at Thirtover near Thatcham has provided specialised facilities. The Guides camp in the open and transporting and assembling all the equipment is a major exercise. They have local sites, but have also visited the South West of England and been represented at international camps. There is some nostalgia as the stout canvas tents that have served the District for so many years come to the end of their lives, but those feelings fade rapidly when the benefits of putting up the modern tents are experienced!

1993

Over the years the appearance of the Brownies and Guides has changed as the uniforms have been updated in line with modern tastes, but much else about the movement retains a timeless flavour. Some activities have been passed down the years, but they are updated with new attractions such as computer science. The challenge and fun of camping remains, and food still tastes best when cooked in the open air. The continuing high numbers of girls in membership is a testament to the appeal of guiding, and a tribute to the enthusiasm and commitment to the many leaders who have given their time and effort to this part of Emmer Green's life for over 50 years.

PHOTO JOHN NOTTON

Townswomen's Guild

The Townswomen's Guild movement has its roots back in 1865 when a group of women joined together to press for equal franchise. In 1928, following on from the peaceful suffragists, Dame Margery Corbett-Ashby formed the Guild to educate women in the principles of good citizenship and in the wise use of their vote. The movement remains non-political and regardless of creed, colour or social status.

In 1952, in Emmer Green, another group of women decided that they would like to start a local Guild. Among them were Mrs Barbara Morley, Miss Phyllis Bone, the headmistress of Emmer Green Primary School and Mrs Freda Morgan, a teacher from Sonning Common. The first meeting was held in December 1952 in Emmer Green School hall, with Miss Bone as President and Mrs Morley as Chairman. The first speaker was Mrs C I Smalley-Platten and her subject was 'Modern Flower Arranging'.

Slowly the membership grew and the Guild flourished. The principal aim has been to educate, and the wide diversity of speakers' subjects reflect this. They have included such topics as acupuncture, animal welfare, art, cookery, linguistics, literature, local Issues and music. As part of the national membership, Townswomen representatives are sent to the annual National Council Meeting, often held in The Royal Albert Hall, where topics ranging from genetically modified food, the licensing of guns and legalising the use of cannabis to alleviate chronic medical conditions are just a few which have been professionally debated and often taken further to Parliamentary levels.

Within the Guild there have always been several smaller specialist groups. These change over the years but two very strong groups in the early years were the choir and the drama groups. The choir entertained Guild members and also took part in the many, well supported, music festivals held both in Reading and farther afield, rarely returning without a cup or certificate. An adjudicator at Reading one year was a certain C Lloyd-Webber, father of Andrew and Julian! The drama group too, competed successfully at many festivals and also gave public performances mainly in St Barnabas Church Hall. Mrs Enid Caddy was also a member of Reading Repertory Company and was invaluable to the group, and Mrs Barbara Sidford worked tirelessly as producer. For many years the Guild Ramblers enjoyed exploring Emmer Green and its surroundings, even holidaying abroad. The 'Social Studies Group' spent two years learning about the history of Reading, have listened to speakers on women in business and heard about the different worldwide religions. At the present time the Guild continues to enjoy gardening, words and music and arts and crafts. When the national movement holds a competition or exhibition Emmer Green takes part where possible and for years was also a notable presence at the Reading Show.

Emmer Green Townswomen's Guild Choir in the 1970s PHOTO FISHER COLLECTION

Broadcaster Robert Dougall with the Townswomen's Guild in 1968

Taking part in the life of the wider community has always been important to Emmer Green and members have assisted at the local baby clinic, the luncheon club, the hospital tea bars, the scout shop and various local charity shops. As a national movement members have enjoyed supporting various fund-raising schemes. The first of these was a request in the early 1950s to raise money to build a block of flats in Austria providing homes for refugees from the Second World War. Other achievements include the provision of a new ward at Stoke Mandeville following a challenge from Sir Jimmy Saville and building a mother and baby clinic in Dhaka in response to a request from H R H The Princess Royal. This clinic continues to flourish under the Save the Children Fund. Several new woodlands have been planted throughout the British Isles. Members have 'Walked for Macmillan Nurses' and have helped to pay for a premature baby incubator and a mammography machine for Berkshire.

In 1980 Mrs Elizabeth Risius, the then Chairman, planted a tree near Emmer Green pond, and a seat near Reading Town Hall bears a plaque in honour of Mrs Barbara Morley, Emmer Green's first Chairman, in gratitude for her work in Berkshire and North Hants Federation of Townswomen's Guilds.

For nearly fifty years the Emmer Green Guild's membership has remained healthy although the average age has gradually increased. This is due in part to a radical change in the lifestyle of the nation. In the 1950s and 1960s many more women were at home all day taking care of the house and family and looked forward to an evening out and time to socialise and learn something new. Women of today have increased mobility, a much wider choice of activities and many more varied demands on their time. However, Emmer Green Guild members continue to enjoy a wide variety of speakers and activities offering friendship, support and education and look forward under the, chairmanship of Mrs Maureen Chamberlain, to flourishing in the 21st Century.

The Arts and Crafts Group in the 1980s

Women's Institute

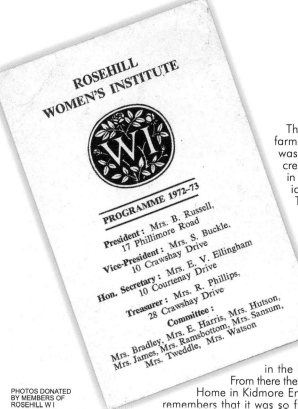

The first ever W I was started in Canada by a group of farmers' wives. By 1915 it was established in England. It was always non-sectarian, non-party political and was created to enable countrywomen to take an effective part in rural country life. The movement is based on the spiritual ideas of fellowship, truth, tolerance and justice. The Townswomen's Guild had already been running in Emmer Green for ten years when it was felt there was a need to meet afternoon interests, by forming a local Women's Institute. The branch was founded in June 1963, by Mrs Doris Robinson, with forty-five members enrolling. It became known as the Rosehill W I and was one of several groups who all form the Caversham Group. It is also affiliated to Berkshire Federation, which is, in turn, affiliated to the National Federation of Women's Institutes in London. There have been more than a dozen Presidents leading Rosehill W I since 1963.

Over the years they have had several 'homes'. The first and second foundation meetings were held in the headquarters of Reading Athletic Club in Kiln Road. From there they moved to a wooden chalet in the grounds of St Benet's Home in Kidmore End Road. One of the original members, Mrs Record, remembers that it was so filthy that they had to clean it before every meeting! They then moved on to the Chapel-on-the-Hill, and later used what is now the North Reading Youth and Community Centre. At its height membership reached about seventy-five, but now stands at around fifty. Meetings are now held in the Church Hall in Grove Road, where some original members still attend.

The current monthly W I meetings take the pattern of a business meeting, followed by talk by a visiting speaker on a variety of interesting subjects. Often these follow a traditional theme but occasionally more diverse topics are introduced, such as 'Everyday life in Moscow', 'The History of the Loo', and more recently 'The History, Costume and Music of a Belly Dancer' was planned. Talks are followed by a welcome cup of tea and a raffle, bring-and-buy; sometimes a small exhibition and a competition based on a particular theme.

A couple of examples include 'Christmas Cracker for an Elderly Lady' and 'Winter Survival Kit in a Biscuit Tin'. The competitions are judged on a points system, and at the Christmas meeting, the member with the most points over the year is awarded a silver salver. A Denman College Bursary is also awarded each year and this is balloted for at the June meeting. At least once a year an outing is arranged to places like stately homes or to the theatre. No member is ever left out, and the group always arranges to visit members who are sick or need help. Coffee mornings are held to raise money for charities and for the Institute's own funds. A Harvest Lunch precedes the October meeting, and a Garden Party is held every August.

The larger Caversham group meets once a year when a speaker of quality is invited, and there is an inter-W I competition. For instance, in 1972 the 'group competition' was for a display depicting a country and was won by Rosehill W I with their 'Swaziland' exhibit, This was later entered into an International Exhibition at Reading Town Hall in November of the same year, and at the Reading show in 1974, and a write-up and photos appeared in 'The Times of Swaziland' in August 1974. When the old annual Reading Show was held, Rosehill always entered the competition for the W I Challenge Cup. In 1975 they entered a competition to depict a famous painting – Mrs Allen models as 'Pinky' by Thomas Lawrence (1769-1830). Another year one of the members, Mrs Gillings, demonstrated cushion and bobbin lace making on the W I stall.

Also in 1972 the group entered the W I competition entitled 'This Green and Pleasant Land?', and their entry showing the threat to the environment was displayed at Olympia, London. Other competitions entered by the Rosehill W I included the Jubilee Cup Competition for a pub scrapbook (Berkshire W Is) for which Mrs Ellingham wrote a history and gathered photographs of The White Horse pub. Sixty-six entries were received and, although Rosehill did not win, they were mentioned as being in the top eighteen entries, and their scrapbook was put on show in Watlington House, the then county HQ.

Rosehill W I were not a group to miss out on national schemes and in 1969 a group of ten ladies (photo on opposite page) participated in the 'Keep Britain Tidy Campaign'. Armed with pointed sticks, sacks and a litter trolly, they set about clearing the area around Emmer Green pond. A few years later a chestnut was planted near the pond in 'Plant a Tree Year'.

There are several groups within the main body – The 'Walking Group' meet up twice a month for a ramble and a pub lunch. The 'General Interest Group' meets once a month to discuss a variety of subjects and arrange visits. Some members belong to the 'Berkshire Belles' choral group, who give their annual concert at Bearwood College each November. Members receive two publications annually- the free County Newsletter, and the 'Home & Country' magazine for which they have to subscribe.

Reading Library holds a copy of an account of the history of Emmer Green, which was put together in 1966 by Mrs Doris Robinson the founder of the Rosehill W I. It includes a detailed history, interviews with residents who were born in the 1880s, as well as a good collection of original photographs. Rosehill W I also contributed an account of Emmer Green to the 'Berkshire Village Book'.

Red Cross

In 1986 the Emmer Green Centre of the Red Cross celebrated its 25th Anniversary, and a scrap-book was compiled dedicated to its history. It began life as the Berks 50 in March 1961, when Mrs Manning Press was President. Mrs J M Fisher, landlady of The Black Horse public house was the first Commandant, but by 1963 life had become very busy running the pub, so she resigned and Helen Withers took her place. Later Commandants were Eleanor Garrard, Liz Aldersley and Pauline Dent.

They have had several homes since they set up. In the early years members assembled in Emmer Green Primary School hall, but for economic reasons moved to Caversham Hill Chapel, before finally settling in St Barnabas Church Hall. Men joined in 1977, and a total membership peak of around 40 was reached in 1983. The junior, or cadet section was well attended with youngsters keen to learn new skills and doing well in examinations. In recent years the youth group has disbanded and the main group meets at the branch HQ in Reading. All members became fully trained in first aid, home nursing and infant welfare. Proficiency exams were taken every three years. Once qualified they went on duty in local hospitals, to field events or large gatherings, such as the Ascot Races, and supported victims of rail and flood disasters. They were also qualified to carry out instruction to other groups, such as those in the workplace, or Guides and Scouts

To broaden their experience and make training more realistic, members of the group have taken part in special Red cross 'Crash Points' and 'Casualty Simulation' events. These were set up with injured people being provided by volunteer actors from the Casualties Union, who realistically re-enacted scenes of carnage and hysteria. One such 'accident' was staged at a railway siding at Theale, and British Rail loaned the Red Cross three empty carriages. About forty-five members took part, including a contingent from Emmer Green. Another such incident was organised by Emmer Green division of the Red Cross in Englefield Park to help train the newer members about possible injuries to spectators and riders at a horse trial. Occasionally surprise mock-ups of accidents are held at regular meetings, just to prepare the volunteers for the unexpected.

As numbers and support increased over the years a programme of social events was introduced, and this helped to re-inforce the general camaraderie and team spirit.

Grand Proficiency Presentations 1990
PHOTO COURTESY OF READING NEWSPAPER GROUP

25th Anniversary 1986
PHOTO DONATED BY MRS E BARNETT

20th Century War

In memory of Emmer Green residents who gave their lives in the First and Second World Wars. Also remembered are the former St Benet's boys who gave their lives serving with the Canadian forces.

1914-1918

G. Allum

W. Bew

R. H. Bonner

A. E. Briant

R. B. Briant

F. Chamberlain

E. Cox

E. L. Davies M. M.

H. A. Havell

W. G. Herbert

W. Perry

C. Pitcher

H. C. Ryder

E. W. Sarney

A. J. Shailes

R. Squires

T. Tarrant

R. Timberlake

G. Venn

1939-1945

G. Briant

G. E. Bryan

T. W. Christopher

A. Constable

D. F. Dunn

P. R. R. Elford

E. J. Grant

R. G. Hulse

C. Kent

K. N. Lane

D. Perren

C. Pratt

W. Snow

J. A. Sword

Margaret Thackeray

R. F. C. Weallens

A. E. Wheeler

N. H. Wheeler

H. B. Willett

H. J. Williams

W. Witchelo

First and Second World Wars

War was declared on Germany on 4th August 1914. There was a lot of support for the war, and young men were enthusiastic to join the fighting forces. On October 17th the Reading Standard reported "Of the small population of Emmer Green about fifty have responded to their country's call". At around the same time there were reports in the school log of teams of children going to Caversham Park to "gather chestnuts for munitions". This was done several times. Mr William Chamberlain who lived in Fisher's Cottages was a member of one of the earliest submarine crews. Part of Caversham Park was used as a convalescent home for wounded servicemen. After the war was over there was a special victory parade in the village.

PHOTO HIGHDOWN COLLECTION

PHOTO BERKSHIRE RECORD OFFICE - THE MARY KIFT COLLECTION

Although much effort was put into supporting the 1914-1918 war, and any family with members on active service would have been under stress, the next war, declared 3rd September 1939, brought defences and involvement to home terrritory. A heavy anti-aircraft gun was located at Tanners Farm on the borders of Tokers Green and Emmer Green. The search lights could be clearly seen crossing the sky. From 1943 until the end of the war, the field opposite Caversham Hill Chapel was covered in huge wooden crates, covered in tarpaulins. These were apparently U S Army military hardware supplies. A small shed in the middle of the field was staffed by about six U S servicemen. It is likely that this had a connection with the BBC Monitoring Service. A concrete machine-gun post was constructed near the junction of Peppard Road and Surley Row. It was kept for a while after the war, but subsequent neglect led to it being earthed over. The grassed mound remains today. There was an air-raid siren, originally placed on Caversham Grove House, which was moved to the old school, which was at that time a Highways Depot, at the corner of School Lane and Grove Road. Emergency fire engines were kept in the tithe barn at Caversham Grove. The White Horse became a place of refuge during the war, although sadly beer shortages were common. It provided shelter for firemen and air-raid wardens and the Home Guard. Like everyone else in Britain the locals would have been subject to rationing, and obliged to adopt voluntary posts to serve the war effort. As well as the services described on the opposite page, locals were assigned to the local police and fire services.

Emmer Green probably seemed like a peaceful haven to those fighting abroad in the 1940s, or affected by the Blitz. Most of the young men were on active service, or those ineligible were seconded to the Home Guard or became ARP wardens. The local ARP post was situated in a barn behind Grove Farm owned by Colonel and Mrs Stevens. It had basic equipment including a telephone, stirrup pumps & buckets. Colonel Stevens was the air-raid warden in charge, whilst Messrs Povey, Page and Goodworth were three of the wardens.

PHOTO GIBBS COLLECTION

PHOTO DONATED BY CHRISTINE HARDIE

Platoon No 15 (pictured above), the Emmer Green Home Guard included several members of the Salvation Army stationed at Rosehill House, the landlord of The Black Horse, a bank manager and an undertaker who worked at Heelas. The Home Guard base was a chicken hut, part of Park Farm. One night a home guardsman on duty heard a rustling outside the hut. Fearing the worst, he challenged with the call "Who goes there?" There was no response and in the darkness a volley of ammunition was fired. The next day a dead cow was discovered. The local commander, Colonel Field was furious!

The BBC Monitoring Station at Caversham Park played a vital, secretive rôle during the war (see p 90), from 1943, receiving broadcasts from all over the world. People of many nationalities were enlisted and brought to Emmer Green as translators, and they were billeted compulsorily on any house that had a spare room. The payment for providing a room with bed and bath was 5/- per week. There was also a 'V' Detachment BBC Home Guard (pictured right) attached to the 7th Berkshire Battalion HQ. A force of 130 men was lead by Captain F W Skimkiss and at least 50% of the detachment were not British, and included Russians, Czechs, Austrians and Hungarians.

PHOTO COURTESY OF THE BBC

115

The Emmer Green Bombs

Emmer Green was not without incident. Nine high explosive bombs, and a delayed action bomb were dropped from a lone German plane on October 9th 1940, which was probably unloading before returning home. They fell in a line north of the Emmer Green Garage, across Fisher's Cottages and Kidmore End Road, and the last one on part of the Reading Golf Club.

There were no casualties, but Mr and Mrs Tubb and their small rough-haired terrier, who lived in a modern semi-detached house *(photo right)* on the Peppard Road had a miraculous escape. Mr Tubb heard the explosion, leant out of his window to consult his neighbour, only to be told it had fallen in his own front garden. He rushed outside to find a huge crater and to see that his garden wall had disappeared. Mr Tubb's windows had all been protected with adhesive material, so no glass was broken, and although the water and gas supplies were cut off, the house was not damaged.

An unexploded bomb fell into soft earth in one of the gardens in Kidmore End Road. The bomb disposal

PHOTOS READING LIBRARY SERVICES

squad arrived to confirm that fifteen feet below ground was indeed a live shell. Digging was begun to attempt to reach the bomb, and a mountain of earth piled alongside. Work was abandoned for the weekend leaving the residents to fend for themselves. A tremble was felt in nearby houses on the Sunday and they all dashed out to see in fact that the bomb had exploded and created a huge cavern. The bomb squad returned to find their job done for them, and left the residents to fill in the hole. No-one rushed to do this, and gradually the hole filled with water. This provided a convenient resting place for a dead pig belonging to the next-door neighbour. It had died suddenly of unknown causes, so the family couldn't eat it. It took four strong men to drag it to the hole, but to their horror the air-filled pig just floated on the surface. This prompted several days of abdomen prodding with an iron pole to try and release the gases, until eventually the beast sank to its watery grave. Nearly sixty years later that pig was to get its own revenge when suddenly the hole re-opened devouring the garden shed and its contents!

More severely affected was St Benet's Home, where the bomb exploded with such force, that a large building used as a gymnasium was shifted six inches on its foundations. The front wall was wrecked and complete window frames torn out *(photo left)*. Mr T L Flood, the Superintendent, and his staff heard the plane circling overhead, and managed to get the thirty boys safely down to the cellar shelter. None of them was hurt, and indeed the youngsters thought it a great adventure.

The bomb that dropped near the clubhouse of the golf course caused a tremendous noise when it exploded, but thankfully the only damage was broken shop windows and a hole in the roof. The nearby house of the professional was untouched, but by some freak, a blast of air had opened all the cupboard doors.

Evacuees were cared for in Emmer Green, as families moved out of the East End of London to escape the Blitz. Many of the children had never seen green fields or woods before, and although most grew to like it many couldn't wait to get back to London. As Reading's population grew, in the early years of the war, temporary homes called 'pre-fabs' were erected, on the land between Grove Cottages and Grove Road. These homes were very popular and a warm community spirit developed. They were eventually demolished in the 1970s to make way for Pinetree Court, and the houses along Grove Road.

A building next to Caversham Park House was converted into a rifle range at the end of the war, and used for many years by the **Emmer Green Old Comrades Association Rifle Club**. There was an annual shooting competition, and Gordon Page was assigned to use his calligraphy skills on the winner's scroll. He got used to writing one name in particular, that of a Mr A J Boulter!

The patronage of The White Horse by two army generals led to the formation of a local branch of the **Royal British Legion** with its headquarters at the inn. For many years it operated under the chairmanship of Mr Verdin, and at one time Richard Vanderpump was secretary. The band would march to St Barnabas Church on Armistice Day. Throughout the 1950s they helped to organise the fêtes at Emmer Green park.

Change and the Future

The transformation of Emmer Green particularly over the last one hundred years has been echoed throughout Britain. Its proximity to Reading which has also grown dramatically, made its change to suburbia unavoidable. This book has attempted to catalogue most of those developments and unearth some of the surprises from the past. Community spirit might not be so obviously evident today but Emmer Green remains a very active place with plenty of local support for church, schools, shops, pubs, clubs etc. Whilst the future cannot be guaranteed, and most land for housing within Emmer Green has now been used up, one must presume the rate of change will slow. Reading is just a bus-ride away, but our most precious gift is the open countryside of South Oxfordshire. Before the route of the M4 south of Reading was finally chosen in the late 1960s, a more northerly path skirting Emmer Green was a serious option. Had that gone ahead it would have had a serious impact on the whole area. Latterly people have come to realise how precious the nearby countryside is and any attempt to infiltrate what is left is actively resisted. There has been pressure for many years for a third Thames crossing, and opinion is divided on the consequenses of this action.

PHOTO COURTESY OF READING NEWSPAPERS

Little did Captain Maitland realise that when he caused such excitement when he landed at Rosehill House in his balloon in the early 1900s that the children of Emmer Green would be captivated by a similar event some hundred years later. It arrived at The Hill School in 2001 as part of a nationwide programme to teach pupils about the science and history of ballooning, and the importance of maps in everyday life. Many of the changes which have occurred here over the last century we now take for granted, but Emmer Green is lucky to have three enterprising schools which offer opportunity and wide ranging experience to all pupils. These children are our future. They may not stay in Emmer Green, but they should have fond memories of it.

Emmer Green Residents' Association

It often takes a local threat or crisis to act as a catalyst in the setting up of a group, and Emmer Green was no exception. It was a local beauty spot, the Hemdean Valley, shared with Caversham, that turned out to be a focus of unity in an attempt to save it. In early 1984 residents in Emmer Green were officially made aware that plans were about to be submitted by Higgs and Hill for a major development. The threat that over 500 houses were to be built caused considerable concern to the local community. Reading Borough Council opposed the plans and to strengthen their position suggested setting up a residents' association in Emmer Green. A meeting was hastily convened and a packed audience gathered in St Barnabas Church Hall. Caversham and District Residents' Association, already an established group, attended the meeting and offered invaluable advice on the setting up of the constitution. For ten years people fought against development in the Hemdean Valley. Although the building eventually went ahead, the actions by local people perhaps encouraged the developers to be more considerate, and progress has been carefully monitored. The campaign wasn't against new houses, or people, but about preserving something special. Not all of the valley was built on and residents, new and old, are still able to enjoy what is left. The legacy was the ongoing success of the residents' association as a voice of local people.

Since 1984 membership has increased to over 300 households throughout Emmer Green. Eleven committee members are elected at the annual general meeting each April and over the years some 26 members have served on the committee. David Miles has been the longest serving chairman with a total of eight years. Alan Perrin has also served in that rôle, and Paul Gallagher who has been Chairman since 1996 leads the group into the twenty-first century.

The association has been involved in a variety of matters, large and small and is in constant touch with Reading Borough Council. It enjoys a close relationship with the Peppard Ward Councillors, in particular Ian Fenwick and Bob Green (Mayor of Reading in the year 2000). A variety of speakers has attended the AGM, including representatives from Thames Water, British Gas, Thames Valley Police, Berkshire Woodcarvers, and various conservation and environmental groups.

An important achievement has been to establish our own postcode area, thanks to the dedicated efforts of Sue Norris. This has clearly defined the extent of Emmer Green, and given it its own identity. An area to the north of the pond has been landscaped and a seat provided. A vigorous campaign was undertaken to restore a footpath through a nearby wood. The group came close to succeeding, but failed on a legal technicality. More recently a photographic exhibition 'Emmer Green Past and Present', covering pre-history to the twentieth century, was held in the Mansion House at Highdown School . The main part of the exhibition was organized and set up by Emmer Green Residents' Association, but about a dozen community groups took part also. A website, hosted by Highdown School, was instigated, giving the written history. The success of the exhibition was followed by demands for a book. It will be the culmination of about four years of research. Future projects include the procurement of a village sign. The fundamental aim is to ensure, as far as possible, that the development and amenities of Emmer Green and district are in the best interests of the residents of the area.

The Committee 2000

Acknowledgements

Research for this book has been undertaken at:
BBC Monitoring Station, Berkshire Record Office, Berkshire Family History Society, British Library, Caversham Bridge Newspaper Archives, Caversham Library, Christchurch Archives, Museum of English Rural Life, Museum of Reading, Oxford Library, Oxfordshire Record Office, Reading Library, Reading Standard and Berkshire Chronicle Newspaper Archives, St Barnabas Church Records, University of Reading, Wilfred Owen Association.

Research undertaken by members of the Emmer Green Residents' Association Committee 2000 (Bill Goodworth, Sue Ballard, Margaret Ormonde, Jill Verran, Brian Warren and others), Arthur Marson.

Individual acknowlegements have already been given. Often the original photographer or donor is unknown. Photographs reproduced by kind permission of Reading Museum Services and Reading Library Services are 'Copyright Reading Borough Council. All Rights Reserved.'
Berkshire Record Office photographs have been reproduced by kind permission of the County Archivist, Berkshire Record Office.

We are indebted to local people who either took the care to record memories or gather information years ago, or who were able to contribute living memories. Many of their names appear throughout the text. There are too many to name here, but particular thanks goes to:
Doris Robinson, for her account of the history of Emmer Green, produced for the WI in 1965. Mrs Esmé Ellingham, and the Fisher Family. Highdown School and former history teacher Mike Macleod. Mary Kift and others for articles in the Caversham Bridge. Alice Hurn for a detailed account of life in the early 1900s. John Davey for information on the Pre/Early Historic discoveries. Bill Goodworth for his knowledge, tireless enthusiasm and support. John Darby for his memories. John Dean. Carey Moore. Robert Price. Ian Fenwick (Geology and Political Information). Margaret Pocock (Townswomen's Guild). Ray Spackman (Cricket). John Whitehead (Transport). Gerald Wild (Golf). All the community groups, establishments and individual families who have provided information for their own pages. General thanks to Paul Gallagher, Chairman and other Emmer Green Residents' Association committee members who have helped towards the publication and distribution of this book. The use of computer technology has made the creation and publication of this book possible.

Index